WHERE *Angels* TREAD

Real Stories of Miracles and Angelic Intervention

LESLIE RULE

Andrews McMeel
Publishing, LLC

Kansas City • Sydney • London

Andrews McMeel Publishing, LLC
an Andrews McMeel Universal company
1130 Walnut Street, Kansas City, Missouri 64106
www.andrewsmcmeel.com

11 12 13 14 15 MLT 10 9 8 7 6 5 4 3 2 1

ISBN: 978-1-4494-0773-5

Library of Congress Control Number: 2011926186

ATTENTION: SCHOOLS AND BUSINESSES

Andrews McMeel books are available at quantity discounts with bulk purchase for educational, business, or sales promotional use. For information, please e-mail the Andrews McMeel Publishing Special Sales Department:
specialsales@amuniversal.com.

This book is dedicated to

Ross Avi Krinsky,

with amazement at your brilliance, admiration for
your courage, and gratitude for your friendship.

Contents

Foreword

BY ANN RULE

I think I've always had an affinity for angels, one that goes back far before I can possibly remember. I have a wonderful childhood memory that happened in Ann Arbor, Michigan, when our teacher picked the cast for the third-grade portion of the all-school Christmas pageant at Bach Elementary School.

All the girls in our class were to be angels who wore long white "gowns," which were fairly easy for even the clumsiest of our mothers to sew. They simply had to stitch up a few seams in white bedsheets to make costumes suitable for temporary angels.

But three of us would have wings! All of us longed for that honor, and somehow I became one of the chosen three. Very lifelike white-feathered wings were firmly attached to our waists and shoulders by gold cords that crisscrossed our little flat chests. Janet Blakney, Joyce Alber, and I were the angels who surrounded the baby Jesus's crib, and it was only fitting that we had wings. If the teaching staff had decided to lower us, wings fluttering, by wires from the stage ceiling, I was ready and willing to do that.

But there were questions of safety and expense. We would hover only in our imaginations and, we hoped, in those of the enthusiastic audience of parents and brothers and sisters.

I still have the photos taken that frigid December night. In most of them, I am peeking out at the crowd when I was supposed to keep my eyes lowered. I couldn't help it; I loved being an angel with wings and wanted to see how impressed my parents and brother were.

Maybe all happy children feel that they have special angels looking after them. My father, Chester "Stack" Stackhouse, was deeply religious, and I learned Bible stories long before I went to kindergarten. I never doubted them.

I met an angel once—or she met me. I never truly saw her, but I know she saved my life. I survived an experience two years before the night I wore—and sadly gave back to Bach School's cache of costumes—my angel wings. I was six years old and in the first grade in another elementary school, this time in Saginaw, Michigan. I was allowed to walk home by myself because there were school safety patrol guards for the first two crossings. It was only two more short blocks to my house. There was one fairly busy crosswalk and one quieter crossing for me to negotiate. Usually there were several of us, and some were older kids in the fifth and sixth grade. But even when I was alone, I knew neighbors all along the way who looked out for me every afternoon.

To me, it was a magical neighborhood. Once, we were supposed to take a pint of "pretend milk" to school for a nutrition display. My mom, Sophie, mixed white shoe polish with water and poured it into an empty bottle, and it looked very real. Unfortunately, I spilled it as I passed Mrs. Willis's house. When she saw me crying in distress, Mrs. Willis came out and insisted I take a real pint of milk from her refrigerator.

Another time, as I passed her house, a squirrel dashed out from her yard and jumped on my shoulder. It was a tame squirrel. Mrs. Willis had raised it from the time it was an orphaned baby. Seeing how delighted I was at the thought of finding a squirrel who liked me, she gave him to me. He was a cherished pet for several years, although he once ran up my Grandmother Hansen's leg. She didn't know about my squirrel pet, and she did a dance that no one could forget!

Along with my squirrel, my milk replacement, cookies, and hugs, I always felt Mrs. Willis would take care of me—no matter what happened.

But it wasn't Mrs. Willis who saved me from almost certain death. As it happened one day in October, all the other kids from Hoyt School who lived near me had left me behind. I wasn't afraid of walking home alone. I didn't know—and my parents didn't know— that my eyesight was marginal. I was nine before I asked my mother why people liked movies when they couldn't see anything but shadows on the screen. For me, it was like listening to the radio, and I could do that at home.

I didn't even know that most people could see clearly all the way across the street. They could read signs! What I had never seen didn't exist for me. I must have adjusted to my myopia, so much so that no one realized I was almost legally blind.

Horrified by my questions about movie shadows, my mother took me to an ophthalmologist. After tests, he told her that I was profoundly nearsighted. I couldn't even see the big "E" on the eye chart.

But that was three years after my angel lifted me out of harm's way. I think it's quite possible that I never told my mother about my close call. I may have been embarrassed. I may have been in shock. I don't remember now.

Even today, I vividly recall standing on the corner of the busy street that I needed to cross to get to Mrs. Willis's block. I'd been taught, "Use your eyes, use your ears, and THEN you use your feet" when it came to crossing streets. And I reminded myself of that every time I had to cross streets.

I looked both ways and listened carefully, and the street appeared to be free of traffic—at least to me. I couldn't see any cars coming. I started across. When I was in the middle of the street, I heard a loud engine and became aware of a large, dark vehicle that was way too close to me.

I still recall the sense of danger I felt. There was no place to run. I simply closed my eyes and stood still.

Next, I heard a WHOOSH and felt a sudden wind that was strong enough to spin me around.

The next thing I knew, I was standing on the opposite corner. I had no idea how I got there. I didn't know then, and I don't know now. I know only that I was safe on the opposite curb. I know something picked me up, lifted me away from danger, and then deposited me, unscathed, on the curb next to Mrs. Willis's house.

When Ann Rule was a little girl, this pair of angels watched over her as she dreamed. (Leslie Rule)

She apparently wasn't home that day, and there was no one else around. I could see a car that had pulled up next to the curb where I stood. I was close enough to see that there was a man in the driver's seat. He put his head in his hands and leaned on the steering wheel, and I saw him taking deep, shuddering breaths. Now, I realize he must have been in shock; he must have come so close to me.

Maybe I hadn't remained frozen in my tracks. Had I darted out in front of him? Had I walked blindly into his path? All I remember now was that he seemed to be greatly relieved that he hadn't hit me. He asked me if I was okay, and I nodded. He put his car in gear and drove away.

Finally, I turned around to walk the last block and a half home.

And, of course, the question remains. What really happened? I was in the middle of the road, one moment completely confident that I was safe and the next feeling as if death itself was bearing down on me. I was six. Maybe I had no concept of death, but I knew what being afraid was.

Who saved me? To this day, I believe it was my first angel. I think she scooped me up just before the black car hit me.

Probably all of us can remember moments when we teetered on the thin edge of disaster. And yet something saved us—something beyond mere luck.

About fifteen years ago, I purchased a creaky cottage next door to my home on Puget Sound and moved all of my records, research, and workspace over there. My neighbors, Vern and Ruth, were close to eighty, and they sold me their cottage and moved to a condominium.

I had enjoyed living next door to them, and I marveled when Vern bragged that he had repaired and enlarged the cottage almost exclusively with things he had salvaged. His inventions were certainly jerry-rigged, but they all seemed to work. His designs equaled any

Rube Goldberg invention. His fire alarm system, however, was plugged into the first of a series of fifty-seven extension cords! I saw the peril there at once, and I invested in surge blockers and new electric service from Seattle City Light.

When I moved in, I tried to be alert to unexpected multilevel floors and to plumbing, natural gas, or other electric shortcuts in my new cottage—but I had no idea that Vern had rescued a discarded heavy garage door and installed it under the side deck, and it was invisible. If you didn't know it was there—and I didn't—you wouldn't see it. What purpose it served, I don't know.

But it almost killed me.

My writing office was on the ground floor of the cottage, and I could walk out the sliding glass doors and under the deck to get to my house thirty feet away. One sunny afternoon, I'd forgotten some notes, and I headed out the door to retrieve them.

Almost instantly, I heard a clank and a roaring sound over my head as something—a wall?—came down from the deck, its sharp bottom edge slicing into the dirt just behind me.

Shaking, I turned around and saw the garage door behind me. Something had dislodged that heavy slab of wood and metal at the very moment I walked through the sliding glass doors.

It missed my head by three inches. If it had hit me, I don't see how I could have survived such a monstrous blow to my head.

Once again, I have no other explanation for this close call than the protection of my angel.

Beginning with two plaster cherubs that my mother hung over my bed when I was a toddler, I have collected angel images. I have about seventy-five now. Every room in my house is under the protection of several angel figurines and paintings. Some of them are expensive statuettes, and some are cheap souvenirs.

Ann Rule at age six, a short time before her life was saved by an angel.
(Author's collection)

I can't say I've ever actually *seen* a real angel, but I have felt the presence of angels. Both solid and as light as clouds, they are all around me.

And they always give me the feeling of serenity and protection. This book, written by my daughter Leslie, is full of fascinating stories about angels. I'm sure you will enjoy it as much as I have.

Introduction

If you were to ask everyone you meet if they have ever encountered an angel, you might be surprised by how many people admit that they have.

I know this because it was exactly what I did when I set out to research this book. I asked bus drivers, bank tellers, waitresses, and doctors. I asked readers who came to my book signings and people at parties.

Although I got my share of odd looks, I also got stories. I came to recognize the flicker of emotion in the eyes of those with something to share. It is usually followed by a cautious smile and a reverent nod.

Most of those I have spoken with who have met angels tell me that the experience was a gift. Many are so honored by their angel visits that they *want* to share and willingly stand behind their experiences.

In some cases the angels appeared as the classically depicted celestial beings with wings and brilliant auras. In others, they arrived in human form to provide help or deliver a message before inexplicably vanishing.

An angel can offer a brief, comforting touch to soothe an aching heart or urgent disembodied words of warning to save a life.

In the following pages, I will not only share details of real-life angel encounters that fit all of the above scenarios, I will tell you of miracles that may very well be the work of angels *or* some other form of divine intervention.

I have chosen cases that offer hope and, at times, fill the heart with joy. Thanks to the generous people who have shared their experiences, I can promise you will come away amazed. I cannot, however, promise you definitive answers.

As the author, I am the orchestrator of this book, of course, but am aware of how ignorant I am when it comes to the mysterious world beyond. This is my seventh book with a mystical theme, and I have researched tirelessly but still do not have the answers.

It is not my goal to convince or convert my readers, and I am not pushing any particular religion. Angels are embraced by myriad religions from around the globe, and I had hoped to include stories of angelic encounters that featured people from a wide variety of faiths. But as it turned out, most of the cases that came to me involved Christians. Those interviewed include Catholics, Baptists, Methodists, Mormons, and nondenominational Christians.

What do I believe?

I believe in God. I believe in angels. And I believe in the afterlife. I believe that God knows our hearts and that He is not as discriminating as some of His worshippers who insist that those who do not believe exactly as they do are doomed.

But I will not tell my readers what to believe. I will simply tell the stories of angels and miracles and present the popular theories about them. I will reference various religions and quote people on their feelings about their faiths and the fact that angels came to them. I do this from the perspective of an awestruck journalist who has had her own encounters and with the hope that you, my reader, will find some comfort here.

A statue of an angel overlooks a pathway on the lovely grounds of The Grotto, a Catholic sanctuary open to the public in Portland, Oregon. (Leslie Rule)

Chapter One

THE MESSENGERS

AN ANGEL CAN ILLUMINATE THE
THOUGHT AND MIND OF MAN BY
STRENGTHENING THE POWER OF VISION.

—Saint Thomas Aquinas (1225–1274),
MEDIEVAL PHILOSOPHER

Stories of angel encounters reach back through time to an era
when our calendars were carved in stone. Angels play a role in nearly
every religion. And many of those who walk among us have seen,
heard, or felt them.

Those who study them tell us that angels come to us for various
reasons. Sometimes they come to rescue us, and sometimes they
come to bring comfort. Perhaps, most often, they come to deliver
messages.

In the following cases, angels employed startling methods to
deliver their messages.

Miracle on the Mountain

Angel literally means "messenger." It is a direct translation from the Greek word *angelos*. Angels deliver messages of all kinds and do so in a variety of inventive ways. Sometimes the messages they deliver are gentle reminders, and sometimes they are serious warnings of impending danger.

And *sometimes* the messages are alarms, calling attention to existing trouble. On a Colorado mountain on a sunny winter day, a young boy encountered a messenger who sounded just such an alarm.

Forty miles north of Aspen, the city of Glenwood Springs sits in the shadow of the Grand Mesa, one of the world's largest flat-top mountains. The slopes are inviting, especially to snowmobilers who are drawn to the Sunlight to Powderhorn Trail. With a 123-mile length, it holds the record as the longest cleared snowmobile trail in America's lower forty-eight states.

It was the middle of the day on Saturday, January 24, 2004, and nine-year-old Keith Winkler was snowmobiling on the popular trail with his father, Carroll Winkler, and a group of friends as the bright sunshine sparkled on the snow.

Meanwhile, forty-seven-year-old Terri Wood was excited about her first outing on her new snowmobile. She had planned a short ride, telling herself that she would limit the fun to an hour. Though she had promised those who cared about her that she would never ride alone, she was eager to try out her new toy.

She had logged twenty hours of riding in the three lessons she had taken and was confident in her driving. At half past noon, she strapped on her helmet and took off, the machine purring beneath her as she rode the weaving trail.

Keith Winkler and Terri Wood both lived in Glenwood Springs but had never met and were unaware of each other as they traveled the trail. While Keith was enjoying his ride, Terri's came to a frightening end.

Blinded by the glaring snow, she did not see the sudden turn in the road until she was headed straight for a tree. She slammed into the trunk, head on, and was thrown over her snowmobile's handlebars. She plopped face down in the deep snow of a tree well.

Stunned, she brushed the snow from her face and tried to stand. But something was seriously wrong. Terri's back was broken.

Buried in three feet of snow, wracked with pain, and unable to crawl to the trail, she felt a surge of hope when she heard the roar of an approaching snowmobile. "Help! Help me!" she shrieked. But the snowmobile did not slow. Her pleas were lost in the noise of the engine.

Terri had landed about fifteen feet beneath the trail and was hidden from the view of riders. Her wrecked snowmobile, too, was partially hidden by the trees.

For nearly three hours, she shivered in the snowdrift, her fingers turning blue. She had neglected to bring gloves and had worn a lightweight snowsuit for what she thought would be a quick ride. Now, she feared she would freeze to death.

Each time she heard the buzz of an engine, she screamed for help. And each time, she felt sick with despair as the riders sped by.

To comfort herself, Terri said the names of those she loved out loud, wondering whether she would ever see them again. And she prayed.

Around three-thirty in the afternoon, Keith Winkler and his group were headed down the mountain, ready to go home. The fourth grader rode on the back of a snowmobile driven by family friend Dave Pace, with his father following them.

When Terri heard the sound of their approaching engines, she was unaware that they were the last group headed down the mountain and that if they passed her by, there would be no one else on the trail until the next morning.

If they did not stop to help her, her chances were grim.

Keith was not alarmed when he noticed the wrecked snowmobile, just off the trail. "I didn't think anything of it. I thought it was an old wreck," he said, adding that it did not occur to him to notify anyone about it.

Age sixteen now, he told me he will never forget what he saw next. A girl of about ten ran out from behind the trees, frantically waving her arms as she called for help. "She looked scared," he remembered. "Her hair was light brown, and she wore it in pigtails. She had on a blue and black jacket."

Despite the noise of the engine, he clearly heard the child yelling, "Help! Help me!"

Keith pounded on Dave's back. "Stop! Stop!" he shouted.

By the time the driver braked, they were about 150 feet past the wreck. The others slowed, pulling their machines up beside them as they quizzically watched Keith.

The excited boy exclaimed, "There's a little girl screaming for help!"

Carroll Winkler was baffled as his son pointed to the spot where he said he had seen the girl. Carroll had been close behind and had seen nothing but snow and trees. If someone had tried to flag them down, he surely would have noticed.

"My dad thought I was crazy," said Keith.

As the drivers shut off their engines, Keith tried to convince them that he had not been imagining things. "I swear I saw her, Dad!" he said.

And then they *all* heard it.

"Help!"

The desperate cry came from the area they had just passed, near where Keith had seen the girl. They rushed back up the hill toward the sound of the screams.

Carroll shouted reassurance. "We hear you! We're coming!" From the edge of the trail, they peered down at Terri Wood. Keith took one look at her and said, "That's not her! There was a little girl in a blue coat!"

But there was no sign of a child. Carroll asked, "Are you alone?"

The injured woman heard the question as an admonishment. She had broken one of the first rules of snowmobile safety: Never ride alone.

She burst into tears of guilt mixed with relief. "I promised everyone I wouldn't go out alone. But I did!"

Keith was confused. Where was the girl? He had seen her near the wrecked snowmobile. She had to be close by.

But there was no trace of her. "There wasn't even a footprint," he told me.

Rescue workers were alerted, and they soon transferred Terri to the nearby Sunlight Snowmobiles Tour parking lot, where a helicopter flew her to St. Mary's Hospital in Grand Junction, Colorado.

As he watched rescuers carry away the injured woman, Keith tried to piece together the odd puzzle. Only one thing made sense. The girl was an angel.

He had clearly seen a girl with pigtails to her shoulders. He would never forget the pale, frightened face. But human beings leave footprints when they run through the snow.

He was also struck by the fact he had heard her shouts. "Help! Help! Help me!" The words had reached his ears as crisply as if they had been shouted during a silent dawn. How had he heard her over the thunder of the engine?

The local media soon descended upon the Winkler family and Terri Wood, reporting on the lifesaving miracle and Keith's assertion that an angel was behind it. "The story was in newspapers and on the TV news," he said, laughing a little about the fact he has yet to live it down. Each time a new school year starts, a teacher recognizes him. "They say, 'You're the kid who saw the angel!'"

When she learned of the extraordinary event that led to her rescue, Terri Wood vowed, "I'll remember that boy for the rest of my life."

In addition to her fractured back, the accident left her with bruised knees and a swollen chin. But thanks to an angel and the boy who was able to see and hear her, Terri Wood survived that frightening day. Though she died young at age fifty-two in October 2009, the miracle on the mountain gave her nearly six more years of life.

The vision of the angel, Keith told me, has only strengthened his faith in God. Even at nine he had recognized the sighting as a gift, telling a reporter, "God chose me to be the one who saw her."

As of this writing, seven years have passed since Keith Winkler met an angel on the mountain. He is certain he will never forget it.

Angels are unforgettable.

As time goes by, we gather so many memories that it is difficult to hold onto them all. They drift away, like bubbles in a fountain, replaced by another the moment they vanish. But there are certain memories that stay with us always.

The crackle of the autumn leaves as you tromped through them on the way to kindergarten. The warmth of your first kitten as she curled on your pillow and purred in your ear. The scent of blackberries cooking on the vine on a hot August afternoon.

And the time you saw an angel.

Maybe your memory is not so good, and you've forgotten the crunch of the October leaves, the softness of your kitten, and the aroma of sweet berries on the summer breeze. But if you saw an angel, you would never forget.

The young girl in the next story has had seven decades to forget, and still she remembers the mysterious messenger she met on a winter morning so long ago.

Home for Lunch

Thirteen-year-old Françoise de Sery was speechless as she stared into the kind face of the stranger. It was a cold February morning in Orleans, France, in 1942, and she had been walking to school when the man spoke to her.

"Gentlemen did not speak to young girls on the street," said Françoise, a retired architect and impressionist painter who now lives in Hillsboro, Oregon. It was considered improper for strange men to speak to female students, she told me, especially during the German Occupation.

Before she turned eleven, Françoise's childhood had been a happy one. Her family was well off, and they enjoyed trips to the seashore, where she built castles in the sand and took cruises on her grandfather's yacht. At home she enjoyed horseback riding and elegant dinners with her family.

But in the spring of 1940, the Nazis invaded France, and her gentle world became a terrifying place. "Many Americans don't know what happened in France during World War II. It was

Françoise de Sery was just thirteen when she met an angel during a frightening time of her life. (Photo courtesy of Françoise de Sery)

horrible," she told me, describing the devastation of the bombs and lack of trust among people as neighbor denounced neighbor.

She always felt her stomach gripped with fear at the sight of the Nazi police. And she was so scared when her father was arrested. "He had been a lawyer and a judge before 1936," she said.

The Nazis suspected that members of the French Resistance were hiding on her family's farm in Sologne, so the Gestapo came for Françoise's father. They took him away on a Friday afternoon, and she and her mother prayed for him all weekend. On Monday morning, Françoise's heart was heavy as she walked to school, hoping upon hope that she would see her father again.

Now, as she stood on the street on the chill winter morning, a man she did not know was assuring her that all was well.

"Françoise, ton père sera là pour déjeuner," said the man.

"He was tall and strong, with a beautiful face and golden hair," Françoise told me. Dressed like a British man in a beige, belted trenchcoat, he looked sorely out of place on the busy street where people went out of their way to blend in for fear of being singled out for interrogation.

The Frenchmen all wore berets or driving caps throughout the winter, but the blue-eyed stranger wore no hat at all. And if that didn't attract the attention of the Nazis, then the bright green scarf tied around his neck surely would. Though dressed like a foreigner, "he spoke beautiful French" with no detectable accent, according to Françoise, who translated his message for me.

"Françoise, your father is coming home for lunch."

His voice was gentle, but she was shocked. How did he know her name? And it wasn't just the fact that a stranger had accosted her that startled her. She had seen his face hours earlier in a dream!

"The dream was vivid," Françoise told me. "And I heard his voice very clearly. He said, 'Your father is coming home.'"

In her dream, she had recognized the golden-haired man as Saint Michael, the Archangel. She had learned about him in her catechism lessons with the brilliantly colored pictures of the angels and the saints.

The dream angel had looked like the picture of Saint Michael, and now, here was someone who looked like a vision come to life.

He delivered his message and then turned to cross the street. Françoise stood, still as stone, and watched him go. A bus rolled by, blocking her view. When it passed, seconds later, he was nowhere to be seen.

His voice rang in her head all morning. "Françoise, ton père sera là pour déjeuner."

She was struck by the familiar phrasing. "Ton père" was reserved for family and clergy, she explained to me. All other people, especially strangers, would use the words, "votre père."

The entire exchange was very odd. She found it difficult to concentrate on her studies at school that morning as she thought of the man and his hopeful message. *Maybe I'm losing my mind,* she worried, anxious to talk to her mother about what had transpired.

She headed home for lunch at noon and made it there at twenty-five minutes after the hour. Her mother was dubious when she heard Françoise's story and dismissed it as a case of an overactive imagination.

"Then the door opened," said Françoise. "And there was father!"

He was missing his tie and his gold cufflinks and had not slept since he had been taken away. The Nazis had interrogated him the entire weekend, but he gave them no information. He was tired and drained but otherwise unharmed.

When she described the man who had spoken to her, her father just shook his head in confusion. He had never met anyone who fit that description.

"My mother did not believe I had met an angel, but my father did," said Françoise.

Nearly seventy years have passed since she encountered the mysterious man. Throughout her youth she believed he was an angel, but as she grew older, she also grew skeptical.

Was the golden-haired messenger an angel? Or was he simply an eccentric man who possessed confidential Nazi information and a peculiar compulsion to find Françoise and share his knowledge with her?

She does not have the answer but told me that when she enters the Pearly Gates she will be sure to ask around.

The messages from angels seem to be simple yet perfectly timed. Though they often warn us of danger, they also help calm us when we wrestle with our emotions. And, as in the following case, they sometimes nudge us in the right direction when we waver on the path.

My Father's House

It was about ten on a dark winter night in 1981 as Nita Bell drove along River Road in Hillsboro, Oregon. The mother of two small children did not normally stay out so late. But she was upset over an impending divorce and had spent the evening at her cousin's home, discussing her troubles.

"The kids were four and two, and I hardly ever left them with my husband," said Nita. As she headed down the quiet stretch of country road, her heart was hurting.

"I was really depressed," she confided. "The road must have been slick because somehow, I ended up in a ditch. I was way out in the sticks. I didn't know what I was going to do."

But barely thirty seconds into her predicament, a slow-moving car passed her. "It went by and then turned around and came back."

She was surprised that anyone could see the car, tipped into the ditch and surrounded by brush. A man got out of the car. "Do you need help?" he asked.

"I sure do!" she replied.

When he opened his passenger door for her, Nita climbed into the stranger's car. "It's not something I would normally do," she told me. "But I wasn't afraid. I felt a sense of calm."

The man seemed to be in his forties. There was nothing particularly remarkable about him. He was of medium build with light hair and a well-trimmed beard.

"I lived in Dundee at the time, and when I told him that, he offered to drive me there," said Nita. "It was a forty-five-minute drive!"

She could not get over the man's kindness. As they headed down the road, she turned to him. "I really appreciate this," she stressed.

"It's okay," he said. "I'm working in my father's house, and I'm not yet done with my work."

It was an odd response, but Nita did not question it. "The whole thing felt surreal," she said. The two were mostly silent throughout the trip, but every so often the driver asked her a question. "Do you have family?" he asked.

Family! Nita thought of her little ones, waiting for her at home. "I realized I needed to take care of the children." She had known that all along, of course, but somehow the simple question jarred her. Caught up in the turmoil of her troubled marriage, she had lost sight of the fact that this was a very hard time for them too. She resolved to put the children first.

When at last they arrived at Nita's home, the Good Samaritan pulled his car up the slight incline into her driveway. She smiled and thanked him and got out of the car. "I walked a few steps and turned to wave."

The stranger and his car were gone.

Nita felt the hairs on her forearms rise. Only an instant had passed. How was it possible that he had managed to back out of the driveway and speed off?

It was not possible!

It was not possible for a human being.

"I knew then that God had sent me an angel," said Nita. In a dreamlike daze, she walked into the house and checked on her sleeping children as she rolled the strange scenario over in her mind.

I'm working in my father's house.

Nita thought she knew who his father was.

I'm not yet done with my work.

Nita was part of his work, she realized. And her children were her work. *Her purpose.*

When Nita told me about the mysterious encounter, I had to wonder whether there was a reason her car slid into the ditch. Was that mishap an integral part of the scenario, planned by an angel so he could deliver the message that she must remember her children's needs?

Nita was not hurt, and the car was retrieved the next day without a scratch.

The curious episode left her with a new resolve to be a more attentive mother. Whoever her rescuer was, he gave her a message in the form of a question when he asked about her family.

And that message stayed with her through the years, for she raised two fine people who are now parents themselves. Today, Nita is remarried and lives in Hillsboro, Oregon.

WHO KNOWS WHAT ABOUT ANGELS?

What do we know about angels? Views vary depending upon a person's religion. Worshippers from nearly every faith believe in angels, though acceptance of their existence is influenced by things such as geography.

For instance, a 2007 Gallup Poll found that 70 percent of Americans believe in angels, while a 2008 Bertelsmann Foundation Poll concluded that 45 percent of Israelites believe in angels and only 28 percent of Australians believe.

Thoughts to consider:

∾ Religious leaders stress that angels work for God and are not to be worshipped.

∾ Those who collect cases of angelic encounters have noted that angels seem to manifest in the form of whatever will best be accepted by the beholder.

∾ Some religious leaders warn that not all angels are from God, and they advise caution in our interactions with them.

Chapter Two
MIRACULOUS HEALING

IF YOU WAKE UP IN THE MORNING FEELING
VERY RELAXED AND LOVED, OF IF YOUR
ROOM SEEMS UNUSUALLY LIGHT, YOU MAY
HAVE BEEN VISITED BY AN ANGEL.

—*Tamar Frankiel,* PH.D.,
AUTHOR OF *The Gift of Kabbalah: Discovering the
Secrets of Heaven, Renewing Your Life on Earth*

Darlene Glover was afraid to leave her toddler's side. Little
Stacey had been admitted to the hospital with pneumonia. The
worried mother slept beside her daughter all night and was relieved
when she woke in the morning to see her sitting up and smiling. The
color was back in her cheeks, and her eyes glistened with wonder.
Her little voice rang with excitement as she asked, "Mommy did you
see the angels last night?"

"No," replied Darlene. "Did you?"

"I heard their wings flapping!" exclaimed Stacey.

Today Stacey Glover, thirty-two, lives in Portland, Oregon, and is a veterinary technician. She still remembers that night. "The sound of the flapping wings woke me up," she confided. "It sounded as if they were circling above me." Though she was too weak to look up and see them, Stacey *knew* that angels were with her and was overwhelmed with a feeling of peace.

The child did not need to see the angels to know that they were there. Their presence brought a love so powerful it was palpable. That is often the way it is with angel encounters.

Those who sense angels may see, hear, or feel them, but it is the tremendous wave of love that they remember most.

The brief touch of an angel can electrify our faith and give us the strength to get through difficult times. In the next story, a woman feared her situation was hopeless, until she realized an angel was near.

Burden Lifted

Fiona Romanko did not think she could bear it when both of her parents were struck with cancer in 2001.

Ian and Helen Macleod were in their early sixties when they were diagnosed with malignancies within weeks of each other. The cancer had invaded Helen's lymph nodes, and Ian's aggressive tumor surrounded his aorta.

"It was horrific. They were preparing themselves for the end," said Fiona, a Sycamore, Ohio, wife and mother of three who recently earned her master's degree in psychology.

Her parents underwent chemotherapy and radiation at a hospital near their Toledo, Ohio, home. Fiona regularly made the long drive to the hospital, while her husband, Kevin, stayed home with their young children.

Ian's tumor continued to grow. "The doctors told us there was nothing they could do for him," she said, remembering her sadness on a warm summer evening as she put the children to bed.

(Leslie Rule)

Fiona tried to maintain her composure, but the little boys fought with each other, and her baby daughter became fussy. "I was totally stressed out," Fiona said. "I couldn't believe all the blows we'd been dealt."

Hoping the children would settle down, she left their rooms and headed downstairs. "I collapsed at the top of the stairs," she said. *How much more can I go through?* she wondered. *I can't take it!*

The burden was too much. But just when she thought she could not endure another second, she felt the pressure of a firm hand on her right shoulder. A wave of tranquility flowed over her. "I had an overwhelming sense of calm," she confided.

The reassuring hand rested on her shoulder for nearly a minute as hope filled Fiona's heart. She knew the presence was an angel and also knew that her parents would survive. "I walked down the stairs and told Kevin, 'Everything is going to be fine.'"

And it was.

Her father's tumor soon shrunk to the size of a dot. The doctors were astounded by his recovery. "They called him the miracle man," said Fiona, whose faith in God was bolstered by the angel's touch.

Both her parents regained their health, and today, over a decade later, they are still thriving.

While the angel was not seen in Fiona's case, one was not only witnessed, but *photographed* in the following story.

Amazing Grace

It was November 5, 2008, and relatively quiet in the pediatric intensive care unit in Charlotte, North Carolina's Presbyterian Hospital. Except for three very sick patients, the rooms were unoccupied. Nurses divided their attention between an infant with a fractured skull, a little boy with cancer, and a chronically ill teenage girl with a devastating prognosis.

The worried families of the sick children spent much of their time there, and nurses were accustomed to buzzing them in and out through the unit's main entrance. When a nurse practitioner glanced up at the security monitor and noticed the figure in the hallway, she assumed it was a visitor, waiting to be let in. Then she looked closer.

The figure was made of bright, white light and shaped like an angel.

If anyone needed an angel, it was fourteen-year-old Chelsea Banton. She was expected to die before the day was over. The doctors had told her family to prepare themselves for the end. But the spirited girl had rallied before.

From the beginning, her life had been a miracle. She was born on Christmas day in 1993, five weeks premature. Doctors offered no hope. The baby, they said, was blind and deaf. They told her mother that Chelsea would live no more than thirty-six hours.

Her family prayed for the helpless infant, and she survived. Chelsea *could* see and hear, but over the years she struggled with serious health problems, including hydrocephalus and life-threatening viruses. "The doctors told us she would never walk," said her mother, Colleen Banton.

Despite her ailments, Chelsea's buoyant spirit allows her to appreciate life's small pleasures. "She likes to go out to eat, and she loves listening to music," Colleen told me. "And she loves looking at Christmas lights."

Though Chelsea could not speak, Colleen saw the intelligence in her pretty blue eyes. She enrolled her in school near their Mint Hill, North Carolina, home and tried to make her life as normal as possible. Her older sister, Kaylee, had always adored her and was worried when Chelsea was hospitalized with a severe case of pneumonia in September 2008.

Complications soon developed, including sepsis, blood clots, staph infections, and a collapsed lung. Hooked to life support, the fourteen-year-old was alarmed by the tangle of tubes and wires. She pulled at them until the nurses secured her hands.

The weeks rolled by, and Chelsea grew weaker. Whenever the doctors attempted to take her off the ventilator, she was unable to breathe on her own. It broke Colleen's heart to see her daughter suffering panic attacks whenever the oxygen mask was placed over her face.

And now, the doctors were recommending a tracheotomy. Chelsea hated tubes. *I can't put her through that!* thought Colleen. She prayed to God for guidance.

Chelsea had suffered for seven miserable weeks, and the doctors offered no glimmer of hope for recovery. Colleen's faith was strong, and she believed God would heal her daughter, whether it was here on Earth or in Heaven.

It was in his hands, she knew.

The decision was made to take Chelsea off life support. It was time, the doctors advised, for family and friends to say good-bye. Visitors flocked to the hospital and took turns sitting with her. As the crucial moment drew near, Colleen and her family prayed for a miracle.

When the life of a loved one is spared, most of us thank God. We give credit to divine intervention, though we don't actually *see* the hand of God. Colleen Banton certainly did not need to see God or his angels to know they were with her. But on the dreary day she prepared to say good-bye to her youngest daughter, an angel appeared.

Smack in the middle of the security monitor, the image of the angel startled the nurse practitioner who first noticed it. She went to the hallway to investigate and discovered that the luminous figure could not be seen with the naked eye. It remained on the screen for long moments as she called others to see. Excited employees gathered around to witness the miracle captured on the monitor.

"It's an angel!" cried Colleen. She got out her camera and snapped a picture. She knew the angel was there for Chelsea. It would either help her to Heaven or heal her. The loving presence instilled Colleen with a sense of peace. She remained calm an hour later as she joined the half dozen doctors and nurses who crowded into Chelsea's room and prepared to remove her from life support.

When the oxygen mask was removed from her face, doctors were surprised to discover that she could breathe on her own. "Her color looked good," said Colleen. "And her stats were high. She was the best that she had ever been!"

Her sudden recovery both baffled and thrilled the medical team. "Everyone in that room was laughing and crying," said Colleen.

Chelsea continued to improve over the next few weeks and celebrated her fifteenth birthday on Christmas day at home with her family. At the time of this writing, she is seventeen. She has grown steadily stronger since the angel's visit. There is a brighter sparkle in her eyes and, *for the first time in her life,* she is able to stand. "I think she will walk someday," said Colleen.

The story of the angel and the miracle healing made national news, with the photograph taken by Colleen shown on major TV networks in December 2008. Even *The Today Show* featured a segment on it. Producers invited a rabbi and a reverend to chat with host Ann Curry about their belief in angels.

Few people are aware, however, that the story did not end with Chelsea. The two other children in the ICU were also miraculously healed, Colleen told me, explaining that the boy's cancer mysteriously disappeared, and doctors were stumped when they could no longer see the hairline fracture on the baby's skull. "Their parents asked me for copies of the angel picture. They felt the angel was for their children too," said Colleen.

The angel made encore appearances throughout the next few days while Chelsea remained in the ICU. "It usually showed up around 4:30 in the afternoon," Colleen said. Some employees, she added, anticipated the appearance and waited by the monitor to see the miracle.

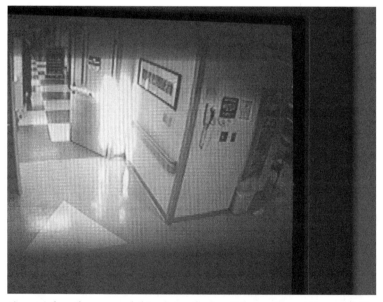

A worried mother snapped this photo of a hospital security monitor on which the unmistakable image of an angel appeared. (Photo by Colleen Banton)

Skeptics have dismissed the photograph, insisting that the image is nothing more than sun rays. But not only was it rainy weather outside, there were no windows facing the area where the figure appeared.

And there is no accounting for the fact that the image could be viewed only through the monitor. Longtime hospital employees could find no earthly explanation, and they had plenty of time to examine the surroundings.

Colleen Banton has no need to convince others. She is grateful for Chelsea's miracle. The angel healed three very sick children and instilled hope and faith in the many who witnessed it. "The angel appearance has changed a lot of people," she said.

Medical Miracles in the News

I CAN SEE CLEARLY NOW

A NINETY-YEAR-OLD Tualatin, Oregon, man baffled doctors in August 2009 when he suddenly regained his sight. Several years earlier, macular degeneration had rendered Martin Alvey legally blind. The retired carpenter had been unable to see well enough to read but could watch television if he was six inches from the screen.

The miracle began when he woke in the night feeling dizzy and called 9-1-1. When he arrived at the hospital, he realized he could clearly see the faces of people five feet away. Experts had no explanation for the sudden improvement in his vision. (Sources include Portland, Oregon's *KATU News*.)

SPARE PARTS

A BRITISH GIRL named Angel may have had a real angel looking after her as she was wheeled into the operating room in October 2007. Five-year-old Angel Burton had been plagued with kidney infections throughout her young life. Eventually, her scarred, failing kidneys required surgery.

As her anxious family waited and prayed, Angel's surgeons discovered something that her mother, her doctors, and the media called a miracle. There, on top of her failing kidneys, was a pair of healthy, fully formed kidneys. The extra organs had gone undetected on scans and took her doctors by surprise.

The healthy organs had already begun their work, and the little girl was on her way to a full recovery without the operation.

An estimated 1 percent of the population have duplex kidneys, but they are rarely detected and rarely fully formed. Doctors say that the spare kidneys will rescue Angel from a lifetime of health problems, including a predicted future transplant. (Sources include *BBC News* and *ABC News*.)

LOVED HIM TO LIFE

IN MARCH 2010 an Australian couple loved their "deceased" newborn back to life. Kate and David Ogg welcomed their premature twins into the world in a Sydney hospital, only to be told that one had died shortly after birth. Kate had given birth to a boy, Jamie, and a girl, Emily, twenty-seven weeks into her pregnancy.

When Jamie stopped breathing doctors worked on him for twenty minutes, were unable to resuscitate him, and pronounced him dead. The lifeless infant was handed to his mother for a final good-bye. With her husband by her side, Kate held her son against her bare skin for two hours, cuddling him and singing to him. She told him about his twin sister and the life they had planned for them. His father also took a turn holding the baby against his bare chest.

When little Jamie gasped for air, they tried not to get their hopes up, for the doctor had warned them to expect the reflexive action. But as the baby continued to gasp and stir, they alerted the doctor and were told that there was no doubt that the boy was dead. When the infant finally opened his eyes and squeezed his father's finger, their hearts filled with joy.

The couple told reporters that the doctor refused to return to the room, insisting that the parents were imagining things, so the Oggs concocted a ruse. They sent word that they had accepted the death and wanted an explanation from the doctor.

Upon seeing the very much alive baby, the astounded doctor could only shake his head and repeat, "I don't believe it. I don't believe it."

Kate had instinctively used kangaroo care, the term for close skin-to-skin contact between mother and baby that not only warms the infant's body temperature but results in a close bond. The Ogg miracle made headlines around the world. (Sources include *The New York Daily News*.)

A beautiful statue of an angel adds a sense of peace to the ambience of a northwest cemetery. (Leslie Rule)

Chapter Three
CHILDREN, ANGELS, AND MIRACLES

WHEN GOD MADE YOU, HE TOLD HIS ANGELS,
"TAKE CARE OF THIS CHILD."

—*Joan Wester Anderson,*
AUTHOR OF BEST-SELLING BOOKS OF TRUE ANGEL STORIES

While writing for Woman's World magazine some twenty years ago,
I was assigned the story of a family whose trailer was snatched up by
a tornado. The young couple had been sleeping beside their newborn
daughter when they heard what sounded like a freight train bearing
down upon them. The father told me how he had held his baby tight
as the trailer was lifted into the air.

The child was ripped from his arms, and the next thing he knew, he woke amidst the ruins. It was eerily silent as his eyes adjusted to the dark, and he began to make out the shapes of the smashed refrigerator, the television, and the debris of the splintered trailer. He found his wife unharmed, but there was no sign of the baby.

The frantic father ran to a relative's nearby home and asked them to bring their car and shine the headlights on the scene so they could look for the child. They had little hope, but as they searched, a high-pitched wail pierced the night. They aimed the beams toward the sound. There was the baby, nestled in a bush. She had survived with just a scratch.

Of the forty-five stories I wrote for that magazine, this was the rare one that was "killed."

The reason?

The editor told me that there had been too many recent news stories of babies surviving falls from the sky.

The angels must have been very busy!

⌒⌒

According to the experts, children have more angel sightings than adults. Maybe it is because their third eye is still wide open, not yet forced shut by the skepticism of grownups. Or maybe it is because the angels *choose* to appear to children but are reluctant to bestow the same gift on cynical adults. It could also be that children see more angels simply because they have more angels around them.

Children, after all, are vulnerable and frighteningly unaware of the dangers of the world, so it makes sense that there would be extra guardian angels on duty to look after them.

The first person to confide in me about her angel sighting was a child. She was my very best friend, and we were in kindergarten in Des Moines, Washington. She was smart and honest, and she

Wendy Yadock has never forgotten the night an angel appeared beside her bedroom door. (Leslie Rule)

The angelic being witnessed in this doorway was seen only once, but was likely ever present. (Leslie Rule)

colored so well that she won a radio when she placed second in our neighborhood grocery store's coloring contest.

I believed her when she told me she had seen an angel.

That was many years ago, but Wendy and I are still friends, and she vividly remembers the angel. "I was five years old, and my Grandma Frida had just put me to bed," Wendy recalled.

The light was still on, and little blonde, blue-eyed Wendy was sitting up in bed. Her grandmother sat beside her, saying a prayer. "I had my eyes shut, but I opened them as she prayed," said Wendy. "That is when I saw the beautiful angel."

Standing inside the room, near the open door, the bright figure was as tall as the door frame. It had long, golden hair and was dressed in white. Wendy could not tell whether it was male or female, and the being had no wings, but she instantly knew it was an angel.

The angel's face was so lovely it was "not of this world," said Wendy, emphasizing that she cannot find the words to describe it. "I looked for a couple of seconds and then closed my eyes again. It scared me a bit, even though I knew it wouldn't harm me."

When her grandmother finished praying, Wendy opened her eyes, and the angel was gone. She waited till the next morning and then shared her secret with her family at the breakfast table. "Everyone believed me, especially Grandma. She was thrilled that I got to see the angel. She was a very spiritual woman and had seen some things herself."

That was the first and the last time that Wendy saw her angel, but the enchanting glimpse has instilled her with faith to last a lifetime. "I have always believed that there is something greater, something more than this world because of my experience," Wendy confided. "I have seen it with my own eyes, if only for a moment. It was a gift God gave me, and it has always helped me through the most difficult times in my life."

Wendy, four and a half months older than I, seemed far more sophisticated than I when we were in kindergarten. She lost her two front teeth before I did, and she could not only remember the date of my birthday when I couldn't, she could pronounce it!

The teacher tested us regularly, and though Wendy would whisper the date in my ear seconds before Mrs. Moses called upon me, her words never made it from my ear to my tongue. "February 25th" was a mouthful for a little girl who stuttered and couldn't say her *R*s!

My baby teeth eventually fell out, I memorized my birthday, and after some speech therapy I learned to say my *R*s. (This was helpful when people asked my name. I was Leslie Mawie Wule until I was seven!)

So I eventually caught up with my smart, older friend. She, however, was decades ahead of me with her angel sighting. I was over thirty before an angel appeared beside my bed. But I will save that story for later because for now we are still discussing children.

While the child in the next story did not actually see a celestial being, she felt its affection for her.

The Kiss

Tricia was happy. It was a sunny Sunday morning, and the five-year-old sat at her grandmother's oak dressing table and gazed at herself in the big round mirror as she brushed her long, blond hair.

Life had been tough on her and her two-year-old brother. Their parents had recently divorced, and her mother had moved away. The children spent most of their time at their grandparents' Topeka, Kansas, home. Tricia loved Nanny and Poppy, but she missed her mother.

"But I felt special that morning," Tricia Seymour told me as she recalled that Sunday nearly thirty-five years ago. "I was thinking about God," she confided. Nanny and the teachers in Sunday school had told her about God and Jesus. With the pure heart of an innocent child, Tricia began to sing as she brushed her hair. "I love Jesus! I love God!"

It was a made-up song, and she repeated the words over and over again, her lilting voice ringing through the house. Suddenly, she felt lips press against her right cheek and heard the unmistakable sound of a smacking kiss. Startled, she dropped the brush and ran to her grandmother. "Nanny!" she cried. "Somebody kissed me!"

Her grandmother listened patiently as Tricia described the kiss from an invisible being. "It was an angel," said Nanny. "It must have been an angel!"

Little Tricia agreed. And all these years later, she still likes the explanation. Today she lives in Ainsworth, Nebraska, is a mother of three, and works as the administrator of a long-term care facility. She does not doubt she has an angel watching over her.

A visit from an angel is a gift. In some cases, it is a gift of life. The toddler in the following story may very well have an angel to thank for her life.

On the Shoulders of an Angel

As Shanna Tuller got ready for bed, she looked in on her sleeping children. It was October 3, 2008 in Pawhuska, Oklahoma, and Shanna and her husband, Robert Tuller, had stayed up late to watch a movie. "It was my birthday," Shanna told me. "I'd put Ali down around midnight, and it was 1:30 when I checked on her."

Ali was twenty-three months old and the youngest of her five children. "I was thirty-eight when I got pregnant with her," said Shanna. "I wasn't expecting to have any more children, but she came at a time when I really needed her."

Shanna had lost her beloved grandmother the week before she conceived her daughter. "I named her for my grandmother, Lucretia Fern Tracy, and also for my best friend, Amber Jo, who died in a car wreck."

She took bits of both names and honored the two women she had loved by christening her daughter Tracy Ali Jo Tuller. It was a big name for a tiny girl. The family called her Ali for short.

Shanna expected to find Ali sleeping soundly, but instead she found an empty bed. Her concern quickly turned to panic when she glanced around the house and could not find her. "I woke up the other kids and we ran around the house, going crazy, looking for her."

They found the sliding glass door ajar. Ali had apparently slipped out and disappeared into the rainy night.

Her hands shaking, Shanna called 9-1-1.

The Tuller family had just moved to their new home on twenty rural acres. Rugged land surrounded them, and wild animals stalked the area. "There were no streetlights," said Shanna. "We were out there with flashlights, searching for Ali. My brother got here before anyone else, and soon we had about seventy people helping us. Rescue workers, firefighters, the police, and neighbors were all searching."

Tears rolled down Shanna's cheeks as she and her husband picked their way through the woods, frantically calling their daughter's name.

"Please, God," Shanna prayed.

No one knew exactly when the child had left the house, but she had been lost in the night for at least two hours as rescue workers combed a neighbor's property. Though they tried to keep their hopes up, some of the searchers thought the situation looked bad, especially after they encountered a poisonous copperhead snake and a pack of coyotes. And someone had spotted a pair of cougars prowling the land beside a big pond.

It was nearly four A.M. when rescue worker Gibbie Gibson, of Wynona, Oklahoma, scoured the area near the pond. "It had been hailing and raining off and on," he told me. He approached the water and was stunned by what he saw. There, in the middle of the pond, was a small child, the moonlight shimmering on her pale skin. She was visible from the waist up, and he assumed the water was shallow as he waded in toward her. But the water soon rose above his waist.

"Ali!" he yelled.

The toddler ignored him. "She was in her own little world," Gibbie told me. "The water was cold, but she didn't seem to notice." Ali was turned away from him, chattering happily as if she were having a conversation with someone only she could see. She giggled and splashed her hand in the chilly water, as carefree as if she were home playing in a warm bath.

"It was the strangest thing," Shanna told me. "My daughter was in a pond so deep that the water should have been over her head. It was as if someone were standing there, holding her up above the water."

It was as if she were standing on the shoulders of an angel.

Gibbie Gibson did not waste time pondering the curious situation. He gently gathered the child in his arms and carried her to safety.

Shanna's heart filled with relief when she saw Gibbie walking toward her with her tiny daughter in his arms. "She looked like a little white angel!" said Shanna. "I asked her, 'Baby, are you scared?' and she said, 'No.' She wasn't scared. She wasn't sad. She was smiling. The paramedics checked her out, and they were amazed."

Ali had wandered nearly a mile from her home, over wooded, rocky terrain and through two barbed wire fences, yet she did not have a single scratch. The soft soles of her little feet were unmarked.

The searchers, however, were muddy, shivering, and covered with scratches.

"You could see where the dirty pond water had gone up over Gibbie's waist. The water left a line on his clothes, but Ali was so clean," said Shanna. "Her hair was still in pigtails. It was the weirdest thing I'd ever seen. I wouldn't have believed it if I hadn't seen it."

Gibbie, too, is baffled by the experience. He has no explanation, except to say, "Something was on her side!"

The water, Shanna pointed out, was the safest place at the time, considering the predators that lurked near the pond. "Cougars don't like to go in the water," she said.

"God was looking out for her," added Trevor, Ali's nine-year-old brother. Indeed, it seems the child's survival was nothing short of divine intervention.

Why had such deep water appeared so shallow around the little girl? Had she been standing on something or found a shallow path to the middle of the pond?

No one has gone back to measure the depths to determine why the deep water rose only to the toddler's waist. If there is a logical reason for the discrepancy in the pond's depth, it still does not explain how the baby managed to stay in shallow water or why she entered the frigid pond in the first place.

How did she travel such a distance over rugged terrain and not receive a scratch? And who in the world was she conversing with when Gibbie Gibson found her?

Ali had been so engaged she did not even turn to look at her rescuer when he tried to get her attention.

Did she have an angel with her? Or did the great-grandmother she was named for help her? Shanna and her grandmother had been close, and she had tirelessly cared for the elderly woman when her health failed. "I feel in my heart it was my grandmother who brought Ali home to me," Shanna confided.

If a spirit or an angel did assist Ali, they may still have been around the day after her rescue. A chill skipped down Shanna's neck when her daughter went to the now carefully secured sliding glass door and pointed outside, her eyes focusing on something only she could see. "She was looking at something and laughing," said Shanna.

Although no one can say for certain who or what protected the little girl, everyone agrees on one thing: It was a miracle.

At barely two, Ali was unable to explain how she survived a cold night in the wilderness. By the time she possesses the verbal skills to accurately describe the strange scenario, she likely will have forgotten it.

The girl in the following case, however, was not only old enough to recognize supernatural intervention, she knew she would always remember it.

Voice on the Breeze

It was a bright, sunny day in Harker Heights, Texas. "I was about four years old, and I was playing outside my grandmother's trailer," confided thirty-year-old Miranda Sky, a Seattle bank teller. "I will never forget that day. The sky was blue, and a cool breeze was blowing."

Her grandmother was inside, taking a nap. "I was allowed to play outside, as long as I stayed in the yard," said Miranda. But she was bored as she rode her red and white tricycle in endless circles on the small patio. There was no one to play with. It was the middle of the day, and most of the trailer park's children were in school.

Miranda gazed longingly across the street at the big, smooth concrete slab that all the kids loved to ride their bikes and skate on. At one time it had served as a trailer foundation, but now the park's children considered it their playground.

"I wasn't allowed to cross the street," she explained. "But I really wanted to ride on the concrete."

Several times she pedaled toward the street, trying to get up the courage to disobey her grandmother, but each time she lost her nerve. Miranda was determined, however, and she finally decided to go for it. "I pedaled as fast as I could toward the street," she confessed. As she neared the road, a soothing feminine voice warned her, "Don't go in the road."

The voice was so quiet, Miranda wondered if she had imagined it. "I decided to just ignore it and I kept pedaling. But then I heard it again."

"Don't go in the road!"

When the mysterious voice repeated its command, it spoke loudly and with an urgency that caused Miranda to freeze. "I stopped on the edge of the road," she said. "An instant later a big, black truck barreled by." She felt her hair lift in the warm rush of its wake. "If I had been an inch closer, I would have been hit."

Shock washed over her as she realized just how close she had come to being struck. "I immediately turned around," she said, explaining that she expected to see a concerned adult standing behind her. But there was no one there.

It suddenly became unnaturally quiet. "It was like time stopped," Miranda remembered. "There was complete silence. There was no sound of birds and no breeze."

She glanced around but saw not one person. "It was a hot Texas day, and everyone's windows were shut," she said.

There was no logical source for the voice. "I had never heard the voice before, and I've never heard it since. It was peaceful, comforting, and powerful."

The voice had definitely gotten her attention, but she wonders how she was able to stop in time. "I'd been pedaling really fast," she said, emphasizing that she had gained so much momentum that it seemed unlikely that she could have braked so quickly.

Miranda Sky has never forgotten the day an angel intervened to save her life. (Leslie Rule)

Miranda suspects that her guardian angel may have done more than warn her. It was as if a mighty hand had reached out and grabbed the tricycle, stopping it in its tracks.

"I tried to tell my mother about what happened, but she didn't believe me," she said. "She thought it was my imagination."

But the experience had a profound effect on Miranda. "That was my confirmation that something is out there, looking out for me."

Her brief encounter with an angel made a lifetime believer out of her. She can close her eyes and clearly recall the sound of the voice of the being who saved her life. Her angel was determined to keep her safe.

While angels are concerned with our safety, they also care about our hearts. They have been known to appear when we are hurting inside. Mae Brewster, who lives in Nevada, Ohio, is today a grandmother but was just a little girl with a broken heart when she got her first and last look at an angel.

When I asked Mae to describe the event, here is what she wrote:

I was about six or seven years old, and our dog, Star, had had puppies. The smallest one died. My brother and sisters and I went out to the corner of the garden to bury it. It was cold and windy, and I was crying because I didn't want to put the puppy into the cold ground.

My sister told me not to cry. She said that Jesus would send an angel to come for the puppy after we had the funeral. My brother buried the puppy, and while he was praying, I looked up toward the water tower and there, on top of the tower, was an angel.

She was very tall. She was dressed in a long, flowing white gown. I can honestly say she was whiter than snow. She had long white wings on her back. They arched up over her shoulders. She stood there, waiting. I was very, very happy that she was there. I was glad the puppy was going to Heaven. I knew that everything was going to be okay.

I looked over at my brother and sisters to see if they saw the angel, but their heads were bowed, and when I looked back up, the angel was gone. It was okay, though. I knew deep down that she would be back.

The angel appeared and stopped Mae's tears. My guess is that angels don't want to see any of us hurting and would like to step in and make things better every time we cry.

But, for whatever reason, we must go through rough times. It would be a weird life if angels showed up to comfort us each time we wept. While they are likely always with us, it is rare when they make themselves known. And when they do so, it tends to be when we are in great need or extremely distressed.

The child in the next story was especially distraught when kind words from beyond calmed her.

A Very Nice Lady

Becky couldn't stop crying. She was five years old and missed her mother. But her mother and father and Nana had all gone out of town. They left Becky and her older brother, Roger, in the care of neighbors for the night.

Becky huddled beneath the covers in the unfamiliar bed as tears streamed down her cheeks. "I thought my parents had abandoned us," said Becky Hopkins, who grew up to become a junior high school art teacher. Today she lives near Memphis, Tennessee, and her memory of the night she felt great despair is still vivid, though over thirty years have passed.

She had been left at a house in New Millford, Connecticut, and though the couple caring for her were very kind, they were unable to console her.

"I remember that I was in a wicker daybed and that there was an upright piano with a bench near the end of the bed," she said.

Suddenly, she noticed an older woman standing at the foot of the bed. The lady sat down on the piano bench, turning her legs sideways so that she could fit into the small space between the bed and the bench.

"She wore a lot of makeup," said Becky, describing the bright red lipstick and pink cheeks. The lady was wearing a dress, and her hair was arranged in tight, orderly curls. "I will never forget the overwhelming scent of roses that accompanied her."

"It's okay," the lady told her. Her voice was soft and soothing, and Becky felt instantly comforted. "Your mom and your dad and Nana are saying good-bye to an old friend. I will let them know how much you miss them."

As the lady's words washed over her, Becky was swept into a deep, restful sleep. In the morning she told her puzzled caretakers about the visit from the lady and then repeated the story to her parents and Nana when they arrived to pick her up.

The adults grew quiet as she described the lady's dress, her heavy makeup, and the strong scent of roses.

Though they didn't tell Becky until she was old enough to understand, the description matched that of her great aunt Annette. Aunt Annette was the reason for their overnight trip. They had just come from her funeral.

The older woman had always overdone her makeup and worn her hair in the same style as Becky's mysterious visitor. At the service, the heavy scent of roses had pervaded the room. Aunt Annette had been laid out in the dress Becky described.

The ethereal visitor's gentle voice had lulled Becky to sleep. Though she came from the place beyond, she was not an angel but a ghost. Like angels, ghosts, too, can be helpful and warrant mention in this book.

I am aware that the belief system of my readers covers a wide range of views and that some believe that the souls of the dead do not linger on Earth. I respect the viewpoint enough to acknowledge it here, but I have a different opinion. I, of course, do not have the answers, but right or wrong, I believe that God in his goodness sometimes allows the spirits of our loved ones to interact with us. It is a merciful gift, offered to us in our grief.

My own experiences, along with those of hundreds of people I have interviewed, bolster my belief. The next chapter touches on cases of kindly spirits watching over us from the other side.

Children and Miracles in the News

A BOUNCING BABY BOY AND AN ANGEL WITHOUT WINGS

TIMOTHY ADDO, a three-year-old New York boy who idolized Spiderman, climbed out the window of his babysitter's apartment and fell from a fourth-floor fire escape on January 4, 2007, and was miraculously caught by passersby.

Julio Gonzalez, forty-three, and Pedro Nevarez, forty, were walking nearby when they heard the shrieks of alarmed witnesses and looked up to see a child dangling from the fire escape in the East Tremont neighborhood of the Bronx.

"Somebody get me!" cried the frightened boy.

The two men raced toward him, praying that they could save him. Just as they got near, Timothy lost his grip and fell, spinning toward the ground as the men held out their arms and braced themselves for the catch.

Pedro tried to grab the child, but the forty-five-pound boy hit him with such force he bounced off his chest and into the arms of Julio. Both men were knocked to the ground by the impact.

Little Timothy suffered only minor scrapes and bruises.

When one of the men insisted they weren't heroes, a reporter quoted an onlooker who asked, "If you're not a hero, how about an angel without wings?" (Sources include *The New York Times* and *The CBS Evening News*.)

DÉJÀ VU

ABOUT TWO YEARS and three months after Timothy's fall, Caliah Clark, an eighteen-month-old Lawrence, Massachusetts, baby, fell from the third-floor window of her family's apartment and was also caught by passersby.

It was March 30, 2009, when the toddler joined in as older siblings made a game of throwing toys from the window.

Across the street, Robert Lemire, forty-five, was chatting on his cell phone outside Mano's Pizza when he noticed the toys falling from the upper window of the Victorian house. He looked up to see the baby dangling as two children grasped her arms. He raced across the street and was nearly struck by a car.

When he reached the yard, Lemire shouted for help and roused Alex Day, who was in the middle of a Bible study in the first-floor apartment. The men, who had never met, managed to position themselves at the opportune moment and caught the baby girl.

Meanwhile, the distraught father, who had been tending to a newborn, looked in on the children and was shocked to see the older kids leaning out the open window and no sign of Caliah. When he learned his toddler was safe, the grateful father told the rescuers he owed them his life. (Sources include North Andover's *Eagle Tribune*.)

ALL OVER AGAIN

ON NOVEMBER 1, 2010, a Paris, France, baby tumbled off his apartment's eighth-floor balcony, hit the awning above the ground-floor cafe, and bounced into the arms of a doctor who was passing by.

The fifteen-month-old boy had been left in the care of his four-year-old sister while their parents went shopping. A horrified neighbor saw the boy's plunge and managed to grab the little girl before she fell.

Dr. Phillippe Bensignor, a general practitioner, was walking with his son, seven-year-old Raphael, on the corner of Cours de Vincennes and the Rue des Pyrénées in east Paris when Raphael pointed out the toddlers on the balcony. At that instant, the baby fell, and the fifty-eight-year-old, athletic doctor positioned himself near the awning just in time to catch the child.

The BBC News reported that the cafe was closed because of a holiday and that employees had tried to take the awning down the day before but were unable to do so because the mechanism jammed.

A FRIEND IN THE NIGHT

SOME MAY THINK that sixteen is a bit old to be sleeping with a teddy bear, but it turned out to be a lifesaver for a Chinese girl in the spring of 2009. The teenager, who lived in Wuchang, Hubei Province, must have been sleepwalking for she mistook a window in her sixth-floor apartment for the door to her bathroom and stepped out into air.

She plunged sixty feet to the ground but escaped serious injury because she landed on her stuffed bear. She had apparently been clutching the bear when she took her disoriented walk. (Source: *Thaindian News.*)

NOT ALONE

In January 2011 a four-year-old Chinese boy went missing for two days and was found alive at the bottom of a dry well with an unexpected companion.

Deng Rui, who lives in Tengchong, in southwest China's Yunnan Province, had missed the bus to kindergarten and was last seen playing outside his grandparents' home before he vanished. His family feared he had been kidnapped, and police soon launched a citywide search.

A friend suggested that the family investigate a nearby abandoned match factory where Deng Rui sometimes played. Though skeptical, they followed up on the hunch, approaching the property's wells as they called out the boy's name. When Deng Rui's uncle reached the fourth well, he was surprised and relieved to hear a little voice answer him.

Rescuers were called to the scene, and a firefighter was lowered down the thirty-two-foot well and attached a rope to Deng Rui. Once above ground, the boy was asked if he had been frightened. He said, no, he had not been afraid, for he was not alone. There was a cat down there with him.

A second trip down resulted in the feline's rescue, but the cat raced off as soon as it was above ground. Rescuers surmised that the cat had fallen in before the boy. Deng Rui had a few minor scrapes on his face but was otherwise unharmed. (Sources include the UK's *Orange News*.)

DRIVING ON WATER

A CANADIAN TODDLER must have had an angel with him when he drove his toy truck into the Peace River in British Columbia on a July day in 2009. Three-year-old Demetrius Jones slipped from his grandmother's travel trailer while the adults were napping and rode his red, child-sized Chevrolet Silverado into the water, wearing nothing but a diaper and a T-shirt. The current swept him away, carrying the little boy and his battery-powered truck eight miles from Peace Island Park to an area near Fort St. John.

The tot's dangerous adventure ended a couple of hours later when startled boaters spotted him. The truck had overturned by then, and Demetrius was crouched on top of it but seemed unaware of the peril. Meanwhile, his frantic family was searching the campsite for the missing boy.

Demetrius was treated at the hospital for hypothermia and was back cruising in his truck later that day and asking when he could ride his "boat" again. His grandmother, Anita Newdorf, told a reporter that the truck still "worked like a charm." (Sources include Britain's *Daily Mail*.)

THE CRADLE WILL ROCK

A WEEK-OLD INFANT was asleep in her bed on January 12, 2010, in Jacmel, Haiti, when a magnitude 7.0 earthquake struck, causing the walls of her home to crash down around her.

Michelene Joassaint, twenty-three, had just put her newborn to bed in their rented room and stepped outside when the trembling began. There was no time for her to reach the baby before the two-story building collapsed. Everyone assumed that little Elisabeth had perished when she was buried in the ruins.

The grief-stricken mother waited in a shelter for the recovery of the child's remains as rescuers combed the widespread devastation for survivors. The worst earthquake to hit the impoverished country in more than two centuries claimed over two hundred thousand lives, and the hope of finding survivors diminished with each passing day.

Elisabeth, however, was discovered alive and still in her bed, seven days after the quake. French rescuers were astonished to hear faint cries coming from the rubble. They investigated and found the baby beneath chunks of concrete. Though dehydrated and thin after spending half her life beneath the ruins, she was barely scratched.

When the child was brought to Michelene, she at first did not believe the scrawny baby wrapped in an unfamiliar blanket could possibly be her Elisabeth. But when she saw the birthmark on her daughter's knee, she cried tears of joy. She said her daughter's survival was "a miracle and the mercy of God." (Sources include Britain's *The Telegraph*.)

UNEXPECTED TRIP

A THREE-YEAR-OLD English girl was laughing and splashing with her six-year-old sister in what appeared to be an innocent puddle when she suddenly vanished. Heavy rains in the area had concealed a storm drain in Riverside Park in County Durham, and little Leona Baxter was sucked beneath the water and into a 230-foot-long underground pipe in September 2008.

When he realized she was missing, the child's father, thirty-four-year-old Mark Baxter, reached beneath the water and felt a whirlpool and the loose manhole lid of the storm drain. He figured out what had happened and raced toward the nearby river. As he suspected, Leona had been carried to the river, where he found her floating face down and not breathing. He handed her to her mother, Beverly, who was waiting on the riverbank.

Paramedics had already arrived, and they soon resuscitated the child. While her skin was badly scraped from her journey through the pipe and she suffered from hypothermia, she was otherwise unharmed. The family, who lives in Leeming, North Yorkshire, thanked God that there had been no grate on the end of the pipe that spilled into the river.

Leona's mother said, "Someone is watching over us." (Sources include Britain's *Daily Mail* and *Yorkshire Post*.)

ANGEL ON THE TRACKS

Two INFANTS came into the world in such a traumatic manner that their survival is nothing short of a miracle. Both babies were born in India aboard speeding trains, and both took their first breaths on the tracks.

The shocking incidents occurred twenty months apart, and each had a happy ending. In February 2008 Bhuri Kalbi, thirty-three, a pregnant woman from Rajasthan, India, was traveling on a train when she entered the restroom and unexpectedly gave birth. The infant, born eight to ten weeks premature, fell through the primitive toilet and landed on the tracks.

Bhuri fainted and was later found by relatives, who pulled the train's emergency brake. Nearly two hours after she fell, the 3.22-pound girl was discovered by a station guard and was rushed to Rajasthan Hospital in Ahmadabad, India, where she was reunited with her mother. Despite the ordeal, the child was cold but unharmed.

In October 2009, thirty-year-old Rinku Debi Roy was on a train in eastern India when she went to the lavatory, experienced sudden labor pains, and gave birth. When her newborn son dropped through the toilet chute, his mother leapt from the moving train into the black night to search for him.

Confused passengers thought they had witnessed a suicide attempt, and someone pulled the train's emergency cord.

Rinku's husband, train staff, and some of the passengers ran a mile to the spot where they discovered the new mother cradling the baby as she sat next to the tracks. The baby boy was uninjured, and his mother had just a few scratches on one arm. (Sources include *The Times of India*.)

Chapter Four

ANGELIC SPIRITS

THUS, ARE GHOSTS AMONG US BRINGING
MESSAGES. I HAVE DISCOVERED THAT THEY EXIST,
MORE OFTEN THAN NOT, TO OFFER AID INSTEAD
OF FEAR. I HAVE GROWN FOND OF THEM BECAUSE
THEY HAVE SO MUCH TO TEACH.

—Author Jack Cady

Jack Cady was a prolific Port Townsend, Washington, award-
winning author and writing teacher. I am sorry to say that I had not
heard of him until the above quote was brought to my attention in a
synchronistic manner.

According to his statement, ghosts are here to help us. If that is
true, then ghosts are a little like guardian angels. After interviewing
hundreds of people about their spirit encounters, I have noted
distinct differences in the descriptions of the two entities.

For instance, many people have told me of angels who appeared as very, very tall—sometimes as large as giants—but I have never investigated a case where a ghost manifested in anything other than a normal human size.

While ghosts can appear as slightly transparent, as solid as live human beings, or as vague, smoky figures, no one has ever told me of an encounter with a dazzling ghost. People often describe angels with words such as *brilliant* and *shining.* A ghost might glow, but an angel can shimmer with light so bright it is not of this earth.

Angel encounters usually leave people with a sense of joy and peace. Ghosts evoke a variety of reactions, including fascination or fear.

There are also similarities between the two. Both angels and ghosts can be helpful. Evidence suggests that each can sometimes look very much like live human beings or animals. And when it comes to meeting either angels or ghosts, people often describe using telepathic communication, with no need for spoken words.

I listen very carefully when people share their stories of spirit encounters. And when they are uncertain about what they saw, I find myself weighing the characteristics described to determine whether the entity was ghost or angel.

I made too quick a judgment when Judy Williamson told me of her odd encounter on a foggy fall night. I at first decided that she had met an angel but soon changed my mind. I now believe she encountered a ghost.

In a weird twist, the ghost himself convinced me, his words echoing from beyond the grave.

Judy and I actually met *because* of a ghost, though not the one featured in the following story. She is a writer, living in Seattle, and a few years back she decided to write a play featuring three ghost stories. While looking for inspiration, she stumbled upon my book *Coast to Coast Ghosts* and was drawn to my chapter "Ghost Trilogy."

As she read, she was surprised to learn that her grandfather, Mokaturo Hori, was featured in the story. His kind spirit is believed to be among those who haunt his former restaurant in Whitefish, Montana. After reading my book, Judy soon contacted me, and we have been friends ever since.

Though I wrote about Judy's grandfather, I was not expecting to write about her. But in the words of Lewis Carroll, "things are getting curiouser and curiouser."

Here is Judy's story.

Helpful Stranger

Judy Williamson felt a prickle of apprehension as she drove through downtown Port Townsend, Washington. It was a misty October night in 2004, and she was lost.

Judy had booked a room at the Bishop Hotel and had planned to spend the next day doing research. It was only nine, and she was surprised to find that the stores were closed and the whole town seemed to be asleep.

"I didn't see any people or vehicles," she said, explaining that it was deserted to the point of being eerie. Other than the few neon signs that glowed in the windows, the shop fronts were dark. She strained to read the cross-street signs as she drove down Water Street for the third time.

"I was just about to leave that part of town to try to find an open gas station so I could ask for directions when I saw a lone old man, a bit hunched over, walking on the sidewalk."

As her car crept forward, the man turned and smiled at her. He appeared to be in his seventies and had a head of thick, white hair that grew past his chin. Reassured by his kindly expression, Judy rolled down her window. "I'm looking for the Bishop Hotel," she told him.

He came closer to the car and stood about three feet away as he gave her directions. He pointed down the road, explaining where she should turn. She was relieved to hear that the hotel was just around the corner. She looked in the direction he was pointing and then turned back to thank him.

The man was gone.

The sidewalk was empty as far as she could see. She glanced in her rearview mirror, wondering whether he might have ducked behind her car. But the friendly stranger was nowhere in sight.

She had taken her eyes off him for just a few seconds, and he had been talking to her the entire time. It would have been impossible for a young, agile person to dash away so quickly, let alone a slow-moving senior citizen.

"He may have been a helpful angel," said Judy. "But when I tell people about it, they think it was my overactive imagination." While she is creative and imaginative, she has certainly never conjured up a man who could give her directions.

"He was so helpful, he was probably an angel," I said. But as we talked, we began to consider the possibility that the man she encountered may have been a helpful ghost. The man, she remembered, had been near the Imprint Bookstore, and he had been pushing or pulling a cart.

"Maybe he has some connection to the bookstore," I suggested.

A little research revealed that a man connected to that bookstore had died that year, and October had been a very important month to him. Jack Cady, a Port Townsend author and college professor,

Judy Williamson stands near the spot where a helpful stranger mysteriously vanished on a foggy October night. (Leslie Rule)

had published a number of books, and some of his favorites were collections of ghost stories.

We also found a newspaper article where the Imprint Bookstore employees were quoted as saying that over the years, the author sometimes stopped in to make sure his books were stocked, and that he had done book signings there.

Judy was startled when she found a photograph of Jack Cady. "That's the man I saw!" she exclaimed. He had died at age seventy-one on January 14, 2004, in a Port Townsend hospital.

Had he manifested on that misty October 26 to assist a fellow writer?

If so, it was an appropriate appearance for the late author, who had said that ghosts exist to offer aid.

Though her experience was a bit confusing, Judy was not afraid. While many of my readers have told me that they hope to see a ghost someday, others tell me that they will be terrified if they do.

I blame Hollywood for their fear. For decades producers have been trying to both thrill and frighten us with their films featuring ghosts. Their methods worked on me when I was a child, but after researching and writing four books of true ghost stories, I am no longer frightened by the idea of ghosts. I am reassured. And I am more certain than ever that I will see my lost loved ones again.

Over the years, I've spoken with many people who have confided in me about visits from deceased friends and relatives. They remember the encounters as treasured gifts and were very rarely frightened.

Susan Walker, from Dallas, North Carolina, wrote to me about an encounter she once had with a spirit who obviously did not want to harm her but to help her. She wrote,

As a young teenager I was visiting a friend one night when I became ill with a high fever. Rather than call my mother in the middle of the night, my friend's mother took care of me herself.

At one point I drifted off to sleep, and when I woke up, there was a woman sitting beside my bed. She was redheaded, with a small build, and wearing a green shirtwaist dress. She didn't speak to me, but I saw a light around her.

When I got home the next day, I told my mother about what had happened. When I described the woman sitting beside my bed, my mother just smiled and told me that the woman I'd just described was her grandmother, who died when I was very small. She had come to watch over me!

This was my great-grandmother Carrie. In later years, we always knew when she had come to see us for a little while. She was a wonderful cook and made, according to my mother, the best Toll House cookies in the world. Whenever I made Toll House cookies, we were sure that she showed up to help us because the flour would fly all over the place! She also loved the scent Youth Dew by Estée Lauder, and every once in a while we smelled it.

People often tell me that they believe their loved ones from the other side are looking after them. Many will say, "My grandmother is my guardian angel."

Can a person's deceased relative become their guardian angel?

While I have found countless cases of helpful spirits who sometimes save lives, I don't know if deceased humans can become actual angels. But I do know that beliefs about this are varied.

For instance, if you were to ask Billy Graham, world-famous evangelist and author of *Angels: God's Secret Agents,* he would tell you, "No."

Quoted regularly in the media since the 1950s, Billy Graham, ninety-two, still offers his views. Over the years, the highly respected Southern Baptist preacher has drawn on his interpretation of the words of the Bible to express his opinion on things such as morals, the afterlife, and angels. He has often stated that angels are spiritual beings who have never been human.

Those of the Mormon faith, however, believe that the deceased can and do become angels. When it comes to the world beyond, millions of people, with conflicting beliefs, are absolutely certain that they know the truth.

I, for my part, continue to ask questions and write about the experiences of those who confide in me. Ultimately, each person must listen to their heart and come to their own conclusion.

As I question people about their interactions with the spirit world, many tell me that they simply sense the presence of their deceased loved ones. Others have actually seen them.

Brigid Reeves, a Poulsbo, Washington, landscaper, did not have to wait long to see the spirit of her grandmother, Dorothy Mae Cullen, who passed away at age eighty on June 11, 1993.

The family had just come from the memorial service and sat eating lunch at the table in the late woman's kitchen in her ranch-style house in West Covina, California.

"I saw my grandmother coming down the hall," said Brigid. "I don't know why, but there was an overwhelming scent of sweet corn tortillas."

Dorothy appeared as she had looked decades earlier as a vibrant young woman. She wore a 1950s-style shirt and shorts and tennis shoes. In the fleeting seconds that Brigid glimpsed her, Dorothy's spirit took a couple of steps toward the kitchen. "She turned right and went into the living room," Brigid told me.

Brigid was stunned. She looked around the table, but most of her relatives were concentrating on their meals and had not been looking toward the hallway when her grandmother made her appearance. Brigid's aunt, however, had seen the apparition. Unfortunately, the woman was petrified by what she saw.

"She put her head down on the table," said Brigid. Her aunt was so frightened that she has never allowed Brigid to speak to her about the spirit sighting.

Brigid's aunt's reaction was an anomaly. Most of those who have seen the spirits of departed loved ones are comforted.

In some cases, the spirits do more than comfort. The ghost in the following story looked after his family and, apparently, the people around them.

Guardian Ghost

When Francis Gould died at age forty-four in 1994 in Tacoma, Washington, he left behind his wife and daughter. But he had not *really* left them. For both his wife, Kimberly, and his daughter, Mercedes, caught glimpses of his spirit.

Nicknamed Franny, he was a Vietnam vet who suffered from post-traumatic stress syndrome. His time in the war was an unwelcome memory, and he felt tremendous guilt over his part in it. He lost his life when he accidentally overdosed on his anxiety medication.

"He was an Italian with thick, curly dark hair," said his widow, Kimberly Gould, a Cottonwood, California, artist. "His spirit appeared as he looked in his younger days, when he was a strong, vibrant man."

Whenever Franny's apparition manifested itself, he was dressed in a white tuxedo. He had rented one once for an event, and for some inexplicable reason he wore it in his ghostly appearances.

The Franny sightings were usually brief glimpses. "I'd see him from the corner of my eye as he was walking around a corner," confided Kimberly.

A few years after her husband's death, Kimberly was living in Amsterdam and was riding her bike when she stopped for an approaching cable car. "I saw a Moroccan woman on the other side of the track," said Kimberly. "She didn't see the tram coming, and she started to step in front of it."

Kimberly opened her mouth to shout a warning, but before she could do so Franny appeared and shoved the woman to safety.

"She landed by my feet," said Kimberly, adding that the woman, in her thirties, was shocked by what had taken place. "The tram passed seconds later, and there was no sign of a man in a white tuxedo."

The rescued lady spoke no English, but it was obvious that she knew she had had a close call. Kimberly could not understand the woman, who began speaking quickly in her native tongue. "I patted her back and tried to calm her down," she said.

Kimberly was shocked too. The spirit of her late husband had just saved a life and prevented Kimberly from seeing something that would have given her nightmares.

The war veteran knew what it felt like to carry ugly images. When he rescued the stranger, he spared his wife the agony of witnessing a fatality.

"That was the last time he appeared," said Kimberly. "I was grateful to him, but it was time for him to move on."

Suzanne Mitchell is another example of someone watched over by a ghost. The Seattle, Washington, radio producer of *The Gary Mantz Show* remembered her teen years when family members saw a ghostly figure in their home. "I never saw him," she told me. "But my siblings and my mother did. My mother told us it was her grandfather, Henry Marugg, watching over us."

At the time Suzanne suspected her mother was just trying to calm them down when she told them the spirit belonged to a protective great-grandfather. Suzanne's parents were divorced, and her mother was alone with three children. It would have been a lot scarier to have an unknown ghost floating around than a grandfather guarding the family.

Henry had been a colorful character. An immigrant from Switzerland, he was a genius who could speak seven languages. "He worked for the Chicago police department as an interpreter," said Suzanne. "He liked to drink and he would go to bars and play the piano and dance at the same time. My great-grandmother had to go down to the bar regularly and fetch him," she said, explaining that the woman grew tired of the lifestyle and eventually divorced him.

As far as Suzanne knew, her mother had never even met her grandfather. So she thought it especially unlikely that the man would care enough to watch over her family.

Then something happened to change her mind. "My sister's boyfriend came over in the middle of the night," said Suzanne. "He let himself in through the sliding glass door and headed up the stairs to my sister's room."

The sixteen-year-old crept through the dark house and up the stairs. As he approached the second floor landing, he was shocked to see an apparition of a tall, stern man. The spirit held out his hand as if to say, "Stop."

The boy got the message. He left in a hurry. When he later told the family about what he had seen, he insisted that he had only wanted to talk with his girlfriend. But the protective spirit apparently did not want the boy sneaking into the girl's room.

"My sister's boyfriend was an artist," said Suzanne. "And he drew a picture of the man he'd seen."

Suzanne's mother glanced at the drawing and got out a photograph of her grandfather. There was no mistaking the likeness. The boy's depiction of the protector on the stairs looked exactly like Henry.

Years later, Suzanne met psychic Dale Brookes, who startled her when she told her that she sensed a spirit around her named Henry.

"That was my great-grandfather," she told Dale. "But why would he be around *me?* I didn't know him! He died before I was born!"

"It doesn't matter," Dale Brookes replied, insisting that Suzanne's great-grandfather was watching out for her.

Those of you who have read my book *Ghost in the Mirror* may remember that I, too, had a psychic tell me that my great-grandfather is watching over me.

Seattle, Washington, medium Skip Leingang astonished me when he told me that a ghost from my childhood home told him that when I was a child I had whispered to him. I grew up in a haunted house in Des Moines, Washington, that (according to my parents) was the domain of the kindly ghost of Reverend William John Rule, my father's grandfather, who had lived there in his last days. I had never told a soul that when I was a little girl I had thought of him as a kind of guardian angel and had whispered to him, sometimes asking for help.

I wrote about the events in *Ghost in the Mirror*, but the story did not end with the publication of that book. One year later, in the summer of 2009, I literally received a message in a bottle sent by my great-grandfather.

It did not travel over oceans but through time.

Seventy-four years, five months, and twenty-two days, to be precise. My great-grandparents put pen to paper in December 1935, and then rolled up their letter, tucked it inside a small glass perfume bottle, and buried it in the rock wall in their garden in Edmonds, Washington. Nearly three quarters of a century later, against all odds, their letter reached me on the day I needed it most.

In June 2009, I was working on the Rule branch of my family tree and after years of searching was excited to find the names of my great-grandfather's siblings. Careful research confirmed that each name belonged to our tree, except for Sarah Ellen Rule, born in 1868. Despite extensive and frustrating research, I could not verify that she was my great-grandfather's sister.

My heart was a little heavy as I decided to delete Sarah from the tree. On the very day I made that decision but before I could do so, I received an e-mail from Susan Moyer. She wrote to say that for years she had lived on the property in Edmonds, Washington, once owned by my great-grandparents and had been suddenly compelled to learn more about them.

She discovered that the Reverend William Rule had been a circuit rider (traveling minister), so she went to her computer and looked online, entering the words *Rule* and *circuit rider* into the search engine.

She instantly found a bookstore's Web site that showed *Ghost in the Mirror.* Because I had written about Reverend Rule in that book, the information Susan needed popped up on her computer screen.

She asked me, "Do you know about the message in the bottle?"

Susan proceeded to share the fact that the Driskills, prior owners of her property, had found a bottle buried in the rock wall in 1978. The local newspaper, *The Enterprise,* had covered the story of the find and published the message found in the bottle. Three Rule relatives read the newspaper account and responded by sending letters to the Driskills, who, in turn, passed all the letters on to Susan when they sold her their home.

I knew nothing of any of it and was thrilled when Susan immediately e-mailed me copies of the message in the bottle and the three letters. One of those letters was signed by Mrs. James W. Evans. She reminisced about visits to the home on the Edmonds beach and riding the Rules' horses to town. She mentioned that her grandmother, Sarah Ellen Rule, was the sister of Reverend Rule.

Sarah did belong in the tree!

And I learned that on the very day I was about to delete her. I learned that because of a response to a message in a bottle, written by my great-grandparents three quarters of a century before. I learned that because (after years living on the property) Susan Moyer felt an urgent desire to research the Rules. And she felt that urge just as I was fruitlessly searching for information on Sarah.

In addition to the impeccable timing and the astounding way the validation of Sarah reached me, I garnered many other elusive facts about the family via the message in the bottle and the responding letters.

I was most touched to learn that my great-grandparents' home had been built from materials washed up on the beach and that when the house was near completion they had no front door. My great-grandfather said, "I will pray for it as we need it for our home."

The door soon washed up on the beach.

Here are the words of the message in the bottle:

Edmonds, Washington. December 12, 1935

This document is placed here by William John Rule, a retired Methodist preacher, and his wife Matilda Hall Rule on the above date. This property was purchased in the year 1910 of William H. Llewellyn of Seattle for the sum of four hundred and sixty-five dollars.

There are two living sons of the family. They are John Hall Rule (eldest). Paul Hopkins Rule, second son. One son died in infancy, Raymond Ryns

Reverend William John Rule lived near this spot on Puget Sound when he prayed for an item soon delivered by the tide. (Leslie Rule)

Rule. John Hall Rule was born Dec 11, 1899, at Chinook, Washington.
Paul Hopkins Rule was born Sept 30, 1902, at Ketchikan, Alaska.
Raymond Ryns Rule was born Feb 11, 1907, at Monroe, Washington.
Died May 6 at Rawhide, Nevada, and was buried there.

William John Rule, father of this branch of the Rule clan, was born in
Camborne, England, in the year 1864. His wife, Matilda Hall Rule, was
born near Mondovi, Wisconsin, in the year 1875. Mr. Rule came to America
in the year 1881 and was later made a citizen of this country. He was
married to Matilda Hall on Oct 19, 1898.

The family have greatly enjoyed living in this beautiful place and have
found the neighbors, the Coomers, the Keetons, the Bigelos, the Killridges, the
Steens, in fact all their neighbors loyal and helpful. John H. Rule married
Doris Grapes who was born in London, England. To them has been born
one son (to date) William John Jr. Paul Hopkins Rule married Hazel Reeve
of Bellingham, Washington. To them have been born (to date) two children,
Robert Reeve and Rita Elain. All bright and unusually attractive children.

These are all heirs to the estate of W.J. and M.H. Rule, still better, heirs
of the promises of God. "Our lines have fallen in pleasant places . . . have a
goodly heritage." Ps. 16:6

Did the spirits of my great-grandparents somehow instigate the
delivery of the message in the bottle? Or was the flawless timing
just luck? Such perfect synchronicity is amazing, yet it seems to
occur often. Read on for more stories of timing so impeccable it is
miraculous.

Chapter Five

SWEET SYNCHRONICITY

WE ARE EACH OF US ANGELS,
WITH ONLY ONE WING AND WE CAN FLY
BY EMBRACING ONE ANOTHER.

—*Luciano De Crescenzo*, ITALIAN AUTHOR

When my agent sent me the check for the advance on this book, I thought I put it in a safe place. But when I went to retrieve it the next day so I could deposit it in the bank, I could not find it. I am not the most organized person in the world when it comes to paperwork, and it is a source of frustration for me when I cannot find a bill or a form I need. But I could not believe I'd been so careless with a check I was counting on to pay my bills.

I tore up my house, searching for the next two days. I knew I could have payment stopped and another check issued, but I did not want to give up. The check had to be there. So I looked in places I'd already searched. And then I went back and looked again.

My niece, Rebecca, helped me. We cleaned out junk drawers and closets, searching. We looked beneath furniture and in coat pockets.

I began to suspect that I had put the check in the recycling bin. And the recycling had been picked up the day I got the check. But that would have been such a scatterbrained act that I was not ready to embrace the possibility. I kept looking until Rebecca said, "Maybe this happened for a reason. Maybe you are supposed to go to the bank on a different day."

I called off the search and e-mailed my agent, Sheree Bykofsky, to explain what had happened. "It's okay," she replied. "I almost never have to stop payments on checks, but I've had to stop three this week." She sent me a new check.

Soon after it arrived, I headed toward my bank, walking on a crowded sidewalk in downtown Seattle. Two dark-haired women, apparently tourists, strolled near me. They were engrossed in a conversation in a foreign tongue. A child of about four skipped along beside them, and they did not seem to notice when she suddenly bounded ahead.

Traffic was heavy, and I grew concerned as the child raced toward the curb. As she was about to dart into the street, I yelled, "Little girl, stop!"

She stopped abruptly, and in the next moment, her mother was scolding her. I could not understand her words, but there was no mistaking the inflection. The child grimaced sheepishly as the lecture rained down upon her.

It was a marked crosswalk, but the cars had the green light and it was rush hour. The mother's tone was suitably horrified.

I don't know if the little girl spoke or understood English. But she had definitely heard the urgency in my authoritative command.

I rounded the corner without a backward glance and continued on toward the bank. I smiled, remembering the frustrated hours I had spent searching for the lost check and then my niece's wise words.

"Maybe this happened for a reason. Maybe you are supposed to go to the bank on a different day."

If I hadn't misplaced the check, I would have taken that route days earlier. I would not have been on the sidewalk the day the girl bolted toward the street.

Maybe she would have been just fine without my interference. Maybe not. Maybe the angels had placed me there to ensure the girl's safety.

It is a delicious idea. Here I am, writing a book about divine intervention, and the very check sent to pay me for it mysteriously vanishes and sets off a chain of circumstances that culminates with a child teetering on a curb, inches from disaster.

Be it divine intervention or an old-fashioned coincidence, the timing was superb.

Colleen Mestnick, a massage therapist in Milwaukee, Wisconsin, corresponded with me about what some may call a coincidence but I suspect was a case of angels at work. She wrote,

I met up with two young boys on my dad's front walk. They had rung the doorbell to ask my dad if he needed any raking done. He said, "No," and sent them away.

I asked them what was up, and they told me that they just wanted to help people and were looking to rake leaves. I told them that I was proud of them and that they were really fine young men to do that. Then I gave them each five dollars and told them to go enjoy themselves.

My dad saw this happen and told me I'm crazy. Then my sister heard about it and said the same thing. I was disgusted with both of them and told my boyfriend. He agreed with them!

That night, we went to an outing at the zoo. As we were leaving, I felt suddenly compelled to turn my head to the side and then look down. There, under a streetlight, lay a crumpled-up ten-dollar bill! Immediately, inside my head, it was as if a voice spoke to me. I heard, "Don't worry. Just take care of my babies and I will take care of you."

It still gives me shivers. I had never found money before, and haven't found money since.

Colleen got back exactly what she gave within hours of her generosity. Was it divine intervention or a coincidence?

Coincidence.

What *is* a coincidence? Some people insist there is no such thing. They say that everything has been planned. It is not up to chance. And if it were, the odds are that there would be far fewer "coincidences."

Others say there is nothing magic about a coincidence. It is simply an accident, coinciding occurrences coming together because of happenstance. In fact, dictionaries refer to coincidence as "accidental."

If coincidences *are* just accidents, that actually makes them all the more amazing. For instance, what are the odds that two children living in different countries visit Disney World at the same time, pass within a few feet of each other, and then meet and marry fifteen years later?

What are the odds that one of those children ends up in the background of the other's family snapshot?

I'm no mathematician, but I'm guessing the odds have to be less than one in a trillion. It happened to Alex and Donna Voutsinas of Boynton Beach, Florida, and was widely reported by newspapers and TV news stations in June 2010. The couple had been putting together photos for their wedding when Alex noticed something startling in the background of one of Donna's family snapshots.

His *father.* The man pushing the baby stroller certainly looked like his dad. And if he was, the baby in the stroller was *Alex.* He and his future wife were a thumbnail apart in the image, forever captured in a square of film.

Astonished by the coincidence, Alex was soon at his mother's house sifting through boxes of hundreds of old photos. His mother confirmed that they were indeed at Disney World the week in question. And there, in the collection of photos, were pictures of his father during the Disney World excursion. His clothing matched that of the man in Donna's family photo.

Click.

In that one instant that the camera snapped the picture, two people destined for love were traveling the same path. The photograph is proof.

How often does sweet synchronicity go unnoticed? Probably far more often than we realize, for such moments are rarely memorialized on film.

One famous photograph caught a moment that was celebrated worldwide as a miracle. On May 13, 1981, Pope John Paul II was in Vatican City's Saint Peter's Square, surrounded by a crowd of the devout. A darling baby in a blue dress, eighteen-month-old Sara Bartoli, was in that crowd with her mother, who hoped to get a photograph of her child with the pope but was discouraged as she strained to see him through the crowd.

A priest told her, "Don't give up hope."

Somehow she found herself near him, and he reached out for Sara. The baby's chubby fingers clutched the string of a big blue balloon as the pope kissed her.

At that very instant a Turkish assassin had the pope caught in the crosshairs of his grim determination. But the coldhearted assassin had one drop of warm blood. He could not shoot the baby. He paused, waiting for a clear shot, but he missed his chance. When he fired a moment later he wounded the pope.

Pope John Paul II was rushed to a Rome hospital, where he underwent five hours of emergency surgery. He suffered injuries to his abdomen, hand, and arm, but he survived.

Little Sara became known as the angel baby who rescued the pope.

She was interviewed twenty-four years later in the spring of 2005 as the pope was dying. Speaking in Italian and broadcast on American television with a translator's voice superimposed, she told a reporter the timing was poignant, for she was about to bring a new life into the world. Her baby, due in April, would be taking its first breath soon after the pope took his last.

Sometimes synchronicity is so sweet, it can make you cry. I learned of the next case via a news story. It brought tears to my eyes. And when I spoke with the people involved, I was all the more moved as more incredible details emerged.

Together Again

Eighteen-year-old Mikey Kuykendall drove his truck down the on-ramp as he prepared to get on Toll Road. But as he rounded the curve, he saw a little white terrier. The dog sat in the middle of the road, blocking his way.

It was no place for an animal! Mikey knew he had to do something or the dog would be hit. Before he could take action he heard the sudden shriek of an approaching ambulance. The startled dog ran to the shoulder of the on-ramp, and Mikey pulled over to let the emergency vehicle pass.

Once the ambulance was safely past, he turned his attention back to the terrier who lingered nearby. Mikey opened the driver's door. The dog did not need a formal invitation. He hopped up into the truck.

"It was like he knew me," Mikey said. He had no inkling that the ambulance had any connection to the terrier.

It was Saturday, November 27, and the vehicle was hurrying toward the scene of a car accident. Brad and Jessika Tetting were soon loaded into the ambulance and rushed to the hospital. Brad had a collapsed lung and broken ribs, and Jessika suffered from a concussion, cuts to her head and face, and a broken finger.

A miraculous sequence of events reunited Wesley with his people. (Photo by Jessika Tetting)

They were uncomfortable, but they were not thinking of themselves. They were worried about their dog, Wesley.

"Brad didn't think that Wesley survived the accident," Jessika told me.

The West Highland terrier had been on her lap when the young couple's car collided with another vehicle on Elkhart County, Indiana's busy Toll Road. When their car crumpled, Jessika had been trapped in her seat. She didn't know what happened to her pet, but witnesses had said they'd seen him jump out of the car.

Wesley was not just a member of their family, he was also Brad's companion dog. The Iraq war veteran had been injured overseas, and the four-year-old terrier was his therapy dog. He sometimes joked that Wesley was "like Prozac with paws."

Was Wesley gone forever?

Jessika did not want to give up hope.

"I had my phone with me, and I kept it on all night," she said. She listened for the phone, wishing that someone would call with good news as she prayed that Wesley was okay.

But as the hours slipped by, she grew discouraged. If Wesley had survived the accident, it meant he was loose on the highway. And it was cold out, with temperatures dipping below freezing. It did not look good for her beloved pet.

When Mikey called his mother to tell her that he had found a dog, she said that they couldn't keep him, reminding him that their shih tzu was territorial and would never accept another dog.

But the teenager wasn't planning on keeping the terrier, though he was quite taken with him. The dog already had a home. His collar jingled with metal tags. His name was written in big white letters on the blue, bone-shaped tag. *Wesley.*

Mikey had tried to call the out-of-state numbers but was unable to reach Wesley's owners. He would keep trying. In the meantime, he knew the well-mannered dog would be welcome at his family's Thanksgiving gathering.

Mikey's huge extended family always celebrated Thanksgiving the Saturday after the official holiday. The event was held at Mikey's aunt's house, a few miles from his Elkhart, Indiana, home. He had been on his way to the dinner when he found Wesley.

Mikey's mother had had to work, and she missed the celebration. All the relatives were impressed with Wesley's manners, and Mikey wanted his mother to meet him too. So after a long workday on her feet, Mrs. Kuykendall met Wesley when Mikey brought him home.

"I was charmed," she told me. "He was so well behaved."

The Kuykendalls' shih tzu, however, was not as enthusiastic, so Mikey's girlfriend, Samantha Adams, and her family agreed to take Wesley in for the night.

Everyone lavished attention on the cute little dog. He was obviously well cared for, and they could see that someone had taken the time to train him. The instant anyone ordered him to sit, Wesley immediately obliged.

Someone was surely missing the adorable dog. His tags said he was from Virginia. What was he doing so far from home? The situation was puzzling.

Though the Tettings were hurting and they missed their dog, they were in good hands at the Elkhart County General Hospital.

The nurses were competent and friendly. As the night shift ended, they were greeted at seven o'clock Sunday morning by a vivacious nurse who introduced herself as Angie.

Angie loved being a nurse. Nurturing was in her nature, and she went out of her way to take extra good care of her patients. After ten years at the hospital, she had seen a lot of patients come and go.

Each one had a story, and Angie wanted to hear it. "I want to know everything," she told me. People fascinated her. Her patients enjoyed the attention and opened up to her. She smiled at Brad and Jessika, who sat beside his bed.

Angie had four patients that morning, and she bustled between the rooms, tending to their needs. Throughout the day she chatted with the Tettings and learned that they had been married the previous spring. Brad worked as a supply sergeant for the army's National Guard, and Jessika was in college, studying to be a set designer.

They had been on their way home to Virginia when they had the accident.

Virginia?

"Something clicked," Angie told me as she recalled the instant the revelation swept over her. She had recently met someone else from Virginia. Someone with very good manners. She realized she had wonderful news for the Tettings.

"Do you have a little white dog?" Angie Kuykendall asked.

Two sad faces turned to look at her.

"Is his name Wesley?" Angie prodded.

The couple stared at her. "We thought he died in the accident," said Brad.

"No," said the nurse. "My son found him. Wesley is fine. He was at my house last night. He's been fed and he's had a bath. He's staying with my son's girlfriend and she's taking good care of him. She lives just a couple of blocks from here."

The coincidence that reunited Wesley with his family astonished everyone involved. "It gives me chills," Mikey told me.

He had found the terrier about three quarters of a mile from the site of the wreck. Shortly after Wesley got into the truck, Mikey drove east, past the wrecked cars and the ambulance with its flashing lights.

The collision had occurred on the westbound side of Toll Road, prompting authorities to stop westbound traffic for several hours while eastbound traffic continued moving at its usual hectic pace.

Within minutes after the crash, Wesley had crossed several busy lanes and traveled nearly a mile before plopping himself down in Mikey's path.

Wesley moved so quickly that he beat the ambulance to the on-ramp as it headed toward the scene of the accident.

After the terrier had jumped into his truck, Mikey noticed a man nearby in a field and had called out to him, asking if the dog belonged to him. The man told him no, the dog was not his, but he had been concerned for his safety and was trying to get him out of the road.

Why hadn't Wesley allowed the man to help him?

"It was like he was waiting for me," said Mikey, adding that once Wesley had hopped into the truck, he immediately moved to the passenger seat and made himself comfortable.

The amazing scenario was synchronized like a dramatic ballet, with each moment choreographed with the precise grace of a dancer's movements. Everyone and everything was in place at the very instant necessary for a miracle to occur.

"Of all the people he could have chosen, why did Wesley choose my son?" Angie asked me. And why was Brad Tetting assigned to her? She had asked the charge nurse that very question.

The charge nurse told her that Brad and Jessika didn't know anyone in town, and she thought they deserved extra nurturing. She knew that Angie would give them special attention, but she could not have guessed how very happy she would make them.

Angie told me she was thrilled to be the bearer of such wonderful news. "It took my breath away," she said.

Jessika had unknowingly left her cell phone on vibrate and had missed Mikey's attempt to contact her. She was so grateful to him and his girlfriend, Samantha, who cared for Wesley over the next few days.

Mikey offered to take Jessika to see Wesley. When she walked in the door, the dog looked surprised to see her. "He looked as if he couldn't believe I was there," said Jessika. "He was so gentle with me. It was like he knew I was hurt."

The terrier usually tended to get excited and he normally jumped so high that Brad referred to it as "levitating."

But over the next weeks, as the Tettings healed, Wesley treated them gingerly.

Angela Kuykendall, whose name contains the word "Angel," was honored to play one that November morning, delivering a message that brought joy to two very sad people. She gives credit to divine intervention for the incredible events that brought Wesley home and said, "Someone was looking out for all of us."

Exquisite synchronicity may be wrought by a higher power. Perhaps the angels are at work, behind the scenes, rearranging events to bring about a desired fate. It is something to consider when we're experiencing life's little annoyances. We might miss the bus or be delayed in line at the grocery store, or perhaps a hem drops because of a wayward thread.

Sisters Rose and Philomena Decicco stopped to fix a fallen hem in one of their dresses when they were getting ready to leave for a picnic cruise on a ship called *The Eastland* on a drizzly Chicago morning. It was July 24, 1915. The girls and their younger brother, Daniel, were looking forward to the adventure but were delayed because of the hem.

The three teenagers were not aboard *The Eastland*, docked beside the Clark Street Bridge, when it flipped over a short time later and dumped passengers into the river in one of America's largest maritime disasters.

Nearly a century has passed, and the Decicco siblings are no longer around to tell the story of their close call, but their descendants are. They are alive because of a loose thread!

More than eight hundred people lost their lives in *The Eastland* disaster. We don't know why so many had to die that day. But those of us who believe in the afterlife are reassured by the idea that the spirits of those lost live on. And those who are here because their ancestors missed the boat are grateful for life.

People who miss a doomed flight or avoid a widely publicized catastrophe are humbly aware of the blessing. Yet most of the time we are blissfully ignorant when we narrowly miss trouble. We rarely learn that if we had *not* been delayed we would have been in an accident. How often are accidents avoided because of timing?

Synchronicity doesn't have to result in a big miracle to be sweet. The smaller miracles of our lives deserve celebration too.

Peg Tabor wrote to me about a sad time in her life. It was the summer of 2005 and the Orlando, Florida, forensic scientist had left her job after twenty-four years and moved back into her childhood home.

The bittersweet memories overwhelmed her. Her mother had died in 2002, and her father had committed suicide on the home's backyard patio in 2000.

Peg was depressed, and she missed her parents. She wasn't sure what to do with herself until she found something to occupy her mind: a miracle of nature.

In all the years she had lived in the home, she had never seen so many milkweed plants in her yard. "The milkweed plant is fodder for the caterpillars of monarch butterflies," Peg wrote. "I mowed around the plants and let them grow. I had many caterpillars show up on those plants. I took a number of them into my living room and raised them through the chrysalis stage in sherbet containers."

When they emerged from their cocoons and flexed their wide, orange wings, Peg took the butterflies outside and released them. As she watched each monarch flutter off into the world, she felt a little bit of her grief go with it.

The perennial plants should have returned the next year. But they didn't. Peg had never seen the profusion of milkweed plants before and has never seen them since. The butterflies lifted her spirit and reminded her of life's beauty.

She ended her letter saying, "I believe that the monarch butterflies were a diversion the Lord sent to me to take my mind off of all the problems I faced that summer."

Sweet Synchronicity in the News

LITTLE WHITE WINGS

A GUARDIAN ANGEL can fit in the palm of your hand, according to the brother of a Chilean miner who was trapped in a mine with thirty-two others on August 5, 2010.

Jorge Galeguillos and Franklin Lobos were driving their truck through the San Jose gold and copper mine in Copiapo, Chile, half a mile below the ground, when their world collapsed around them. Their lives were saved by a butterfly.

The two men had stopped to gaze at a white butterfly, an anomaly so far beneath the earth's surface. Normally seen fluttering around the short-lived purple flowers that grow above ground, butterflies are simply not encountered in deep, dark mines.

As the men marveled at the little creature, the path in front of them was suddenly filled with falling rock. Had they not stopped, they would have been crushed in the cave-in.

Eleodoro Galedeguillos, brother to Jorge, told a reporter that their grandfather had believed it was a good omen to encounter a white creature at night, adding that the butterfly might have been "a little angel."

While the two miners who admired the butterfly narrowly missed being crushed, they spent sixty-nine days stuck in the mine as media around the world focused on their plight and millions of people prayed that all the miners would be rescued. In the end, all survived. Whether the butterfly was an angel sent by God or another case of sweet synchronicity, it was miraculous. (Sources include CNN.)

DEADLY FLU SAVES INFANT

A DEADLY FLU saved the life of a British infant on December 20, 2010. Baby Roman was born five weeks early after doctors ordered an emergency cesarean on his mother, Donna Whatmore, twenty-eight.

The Ely, Cardiff, Wales, married mother of two young daughters, who was nearly eight months pregnant, was worried about her unborn baby when she contracted swine flu. She was admitted to the University Hospital of Wales ICU, where doctors soon scheduled her for surgery.

When they delivered the tiny baby boy, they realized the flu had been a blessing in disguise. Little Roman had a double knot in his umbilical cord, a complication that would have soon proved fatal for the infant if he had not been delivered prematurely.

When the grateful mother learned that the early birth saved Roman's life, she told a reporter, "Someone must have been looking down on us." (Sources include Britain's *Daily Mail* and *Daily Mirror*.)

MIRACLE WHINING

A CHILD'S BEGGING saved the lives of her three siblings and her mother in Brighton, Colorado, on December 15, 2010. The exhausted mother of four and full-time Wal-Mart employee craved sleep and was headed for bed when her young daughter asked if they could sleep over at an aunt's house.

The aunt, who lived next door, had just returned from a vacation, and the girl had missed her so much that she pleaded with her mother to let them spend the night with her. The mother told *Brighton Standard Blade* reporter Christine Hollister that she normally wouldn't have given in, but that night her daughter's pleading finally wore her down.

The pajama-clad family of five left their apartment on Bridge Street and walked the short distance to their relative's house. Within half an hour, they heard sirens and looked out the window to see their apartment building ablaze.

"I believe God was there," said the mother, who called the incident a miracle. The family was so tired, she stressed, that they probably would not have woken up in time. More than a dozen residents lost all of their worldly goods in the two-alarm fire.

ANGEL OF THE BEACH

A TEN-YEAR-OLD English girl was dubbed "angel of the beach" when she saved the lives of her family and a hundred tourists from a tsunami on a Thailand beach on December 26, 2004.

Just two weeks earlier, Tilly Smith had sat in teacher Andrew Kearney's classroom at Danes Hill Prep School in Oxshott, Surrey, England, while he taught a fortuitous geography lesson. The subject was tsunamis.

Tilly knew danger was coming as she walked on Maikhao Beach in Phuket with her parents, Colin and Penny Smith, and her sister, seven-year-old Holly. As she noticed that the water was "sizzling and bubbling," she grew alarmed and warned, "Mummy, we must get off the beach."

Her parents at first ignored her concerns, but the girl grew hysterical. The water, she later told a reporter, was "really frothy" and instead of going in and out was "coming in and in and in."

At his daughter's frantic urging, Colin Smith somewhat sheepishly alerted a hotel security guard about her prediction. The guard took the warning seriously and advised tourists to vacate the beach, prompting crowds of people to return to the hotel.

The Smith family ran for their lives when the wave struck, and they took refuge in their room. While the tsunami took the lives of a quarter of a million people that day, not a single life was lost at Tilly's hotel, thanks to the quick-thinking girl and the serendipitous timing of her teacher's lesson. (Sources include *Sydney Morning Herald* and *BBC News*.)

LUCKY STOP

A SINGLE MOTHER of six didn't complain when she found herself delayed by a train shortly before noon on Monday, January 17, 2011. She had just dropped off a friend and was driving toward the train tracks near her home in Orangeburg, South Carolina, when she spotted a train headed toward the intersection.

Instead of grumbling about the holdup, she pulled over and ducked into a Citgo Quick Store, where she purchased a lottery ticket that resulted in a small win. She immediately reinvested the cash and won again, and then again.

Finally, she purchased a ten-dollar "Carolina Millionaires Club" scratch ticket. She could barely believe her eyes when she realized she'd won a million dollars. The windfall will net her about $680,000 after taxes. (Sources include Orangeburg's newspaper, *The Times and Democrat*.)

TEN-CENT MIRACLE

ONE THIN DIME turned out to be a miracle investment for a family about to lose their home. It was the summer of 2010 when the bank prepared to foreclose on the house where a South Carolina family had lived for nearly six decades.

As relatives sadly cleared out the clutter they had collected over the years, they stumbled upon a box of old magazines and comic books in the basement. They suspected that they had found something special when they spotted a copy of Superman's debut comic, *Action Comics* #1. The June 1938 edition sold for a dime, and its cover depicts Superman lifting a green car over his head.

The family (who chose to remain anonymous) soon contacted a New York comic collectibles broker and learned that avid collectors believe that only one hundred copies of the edition exist, with most in sorry shape.

Their excitement grew when they heard that a copy of the same edition had sold in March 2010 for $1.5 million.

After examining the recently discovered copy, the experts told the family they could expect a minimum of $250,000 at an upcoming auction. A comic broker spoke to their banker on their behalf, assuring him that the bank could stop the foreclosure process. (Sources include *ABC News* and *The Huffington Post*.)

BITTERSWEET REUNION

A TERMINAL CANCER PATIENT and a hospice nurse discovered they were father and daughter in an unbelievable coincidence that had them both crying tears of joy and made headlines across the country in August 2010. Forty-one-year-old Wanda Rodriguez, a head nurse at New York's Calvary Hospital in the Bronx, had not seen her father, Victor Peraza, sixty, since her parents split when she was an infant.

The nurse immediately recognized the name of her new patient and was almost certain he was her father when she noted his resemblance to her. She asked him if he had children, and he replied, "My children are grown. I have a daughter named Gina and a daughter named Wanda."

Overcome with emotion, Wanda ran from the room. After composing herself, she returned to reveal her identity.

The two quickly bonded, with the daughter forgiving her father for deserting her. Victor Peraza told a reporter, "Miracles do happen, and seeing my daughter again was one of them." (Sources include *ABC News* and *The New York Daily News*.)

CANDID CAMERA

A LONDON, ENGLAND, father's hunt for his long-lost daughter ended in an extraordinary coincidence in August 2007.

Michael Dick, fifty-eight, had not seen his daughter Lisa, thirty-one, for more than a decade, and all his efforts to find her had failed. He had split with her mother when Lisa was an infant, and though they'd been in contact at one time, he had lost touch with his daughter when she was about twenty.

Michael knew she had once lived in Sudbury, Suffolk, England, so he and his two younger daughters, Samantha, twenty-two, and

Shannon, ten, took a trip to the area to search. They scoured records at the town hall and the library but could not find an address for Lisa.

The disappointed father sought help from the local newspaper, the *Suffolk Free Press*. A reporter wrote an article about the search, and a photograph was printed alongside the piece. The photographer had unknowingly taken a shot of Michael, and *all three* of his daughters.

While Michael and his two youngest daughters posed on a Sudbury street, Lisa was about two hundred feet behind them. She was captured in the shot, her back to the camera as she walked away. She recognized herself when friends showed her the article. She was stunned to realize that a moment before her family smiled for the photographer, she had been standing exactly where they were.

Lisa no longer lived in Sudbury but happened to be there the same day as her father because she was visiting her mother. The very day before she saw the article, Lisa had told friends that she planned to search for her father. Father and daughter had a happy reunion. (Sources include Britain's *Daily Mail*.)

MIA AND MIA

TWIN SISTERS adopted from a Chinese orphanage by two different American families were miraculously reunited via the Internet in August 2006. Abandoned baby girls are so common in China that authorities did not realize that the two infants were related. They had been left on the streets in Yangzhou a week apart, and no one made the connection until the adoptive mothers met on the adoption agency's Internet site.

Douglas and Holly Funk from the Chicago area and Carlos and Diana Ramirez from the Miami area had, by a strange coincidence, each named their daughter Mia. The Funks had wished for twins and had purchased two of everything but were so charmed by the single baby girl that they were happy to adopt just one child.

The two mothers began chatting online, via the adoption site, when the girls were three years old. They noticed a resemblance when they exchanged photographs, and their excitement grew when they discovered that both babies had been found near the same textile factory. They had the girls' DNA tested and learned that odds were excellent that the girls were indeed twins.

The sisters were reunited at a Chicago airport and instantly took to each other. The families vowed that despite the 1,100 miles between them, the Mias would grow up knowing each other. (Sources include British newspapers *The Guardian* and *The Times*.)

MENDED HEARTS

WHEN AN ENGLISH COUPLE met for the first time at a Kingsbury swimming pool in 1992, they liked each other and began dating. But they weren't expecting to have so much in common. Each had had a broken heart.

Literally.

The pair was incredulous when they realized that they had been born with the same rare heart defect and had had surgery in the same hospital, performed by the same surgeon, on the same day.

Suzanne and Alistair Cotton, today happily married, were children when they underwent surgery at Birmingham Children's Hospital in 1974. Alistair was fourteen and Suzanne just seven when they were treated for stenosis, a life-threatening defect that causes heart valves to narrow.

They recovered in the same ward, spending days in bed as nurses took care of them. If they saw each other, they don't recall it.

Suzanne revealed to a reporter that the two believe they were destined to be together because the defects were on opposite sides of their hearts, and if matched up, "Our two hearts would fit together perfectly."

When Suzanne gave birth to a healthy daughter, Hannah, in 2004, she called it a miracle, noting that many heart patients are unable to conceive.

In July 2010, the Cottons told a reporter they were grateful for their joyful life and were forming a charity called Precious Hearts to raise awareness of congenital heart disease. (Sources include Britain's *Coventry Telegraph*.)

Chapter Six
ANGELS
AMONG US

IT IS NOT KNOWN PRECISELY WHERE
ANGELS DWELL — WHETHER IN THE AIR,
THE VOID, OR THE PLANETS. IT HAS NOT
BEEN GOD'S PLEASURE THAT WE SHOULD
BE INFORMED OF THEIR ABODE.

—*Voltaire* (1694–1778),
FRENCH AUTHOR AND PHILOSOPHER

It is generally accepted that angels can appear as the traditionally
depicted celestial beings with wings and halos or as ordinary humans.
In some cases, what appear to be people are actually angels in
disguise. At other times, angels are simply acting through humans.

I am fairly certain that I have had three encounters with angels.
While each experience was unique, all happened within the same

three-year period. In two of the encounters, the "angels" appeared as ordinary humans, so I cannot say for sure that they were celestial beings.

But one of the experiences was so amazing that I could comb the library's fattest unabridged dictionary and not find words to describe it. As my fingers dance over my computer's keyboard, I realize that writing about my own angelic encounter is far more difficult than writing about someone else's.

How do I do the angel justice?

I do not think it is possible, but I will do my best.

I was living in Lake Oswego, Oregon, about twenty years ago. I had had a conflict with someone close to me, and I had gone to bed with a troubled heart. I awoke at dawn when the corner of the fitted sheet snapped off the mattress beside my head. My eyes flew open, and I was astounded to see a luminous being beside the bed. I instantly knew that I was seeing something I would want to remember for the rest of my life, so I stared, trying to soak in every detail.

The figure wore white, and her hands were cupped over her nose and mouth. Her hair seemed made of golden light. I could not determine if it was cropped short or pulled back. I knew only that it hugged her head and that each strand was dazzling. I was most taken with the curve of her cheek. It was a deep shade of peach, and her complexion shone as if she were lit from within. I was in awe, aware that I was receiving a wondrous gift.

The figure was smaller than an adult, but her features were not childish. She remained for a full four seconds before vanishing.

I instinctively knew that I had seen an angel. She had no halo. She had no wings. Though I say "she" when I describe her, I somehow sensed that although she appeared feminine, she was a sexless being.

Prior to her appearance, I did not know that angels were real. As mentioned in an earlier chapter, I believed my childhood friend Wendy when she told me that she had seen an angel. But back then, I also believed in the Easter Bunny. By the time the celestial being appeared beside my bed, angels were as real to me as mermaids. But now I had *seen* one!

I lay there for some time, contemplating the visit.

It had occurred at twilight, when the last of the night's shadows had seeped away but the room was still dim. The angel was illuminated, a bright contrast to the soft light.

That day, I told more people about the angel than I told in the next twenty years. Some were skeptical, some made jokes, and some believed me and shared my amazement. I was so excited that I wanted to share. I was bursting to tell the story! But as time went on, I kept the memory closer to my heart, protecting it like a fragile treasure.

I have had other mystical experiences and have written about some of them in my other books, but the angel was special. I don't know why she appeared to me. The encounter brought much-needed comfort, but I wonder if there was another purpose for her visit. Perhaps it was so I could write about it and give hope to others. Quite frankly, I would not be writing this book if I had not seen her, for I would be too skeptical about others' encounters to take them seriously.

That may seem strange, considering that I have always believed in ghosts. But I grew up in a haunted house, so I never doubted their existence. When I was a child and learned about God, I was taught that the Bible was not to be taken literally. I assumed that angels were nothing more than Bible metaphors.

Seeing is believing.

It is a cliché, but it is true. I had to see an angel to believe in their existence.

After seeing my angel, I will never again doubt her existence. Now, as I research this book and interview many people about their angel sightings, I have noted that it is common for them to appear beside our beds. The next story is another example.

Restless Night

Beth Lauderdale had been in bed for hours, but she could not sleep. It was an April night in 2010, and she and her husband were vacationing on the Big Island in Hawaii, where they rented the same old beach house each year. "It was raining all night," she said. "I was worried about the cat because she liked to sleep on the porch, and I was afraid she would get wet."

Lava Kitty had been a stray who now lived on the premises. The landlord provided cat food, and the vacationers cared for her. Beth, a Tacoma, Washington, writer, was particularly fond of the sweet calico cat and always looked forward to seeing her during their month-long visits.

Despite the downpour, Lava Kitty was determined to sleep on her chair on the porch, so Beth had dragged the heavy chair across the porch so that it was positioned beneath the eaves. Still, she worried about the elderly cat and found herself stirring restlessly as rain pelted the roof and lightning flashed outside. "I woke at dawn," said Beth.

The storm had settled and all was quiet, but something very strange was happening. There, in the corner of the room was a

Beth Lauderdale will never forget the radiant being who appeared to her after a stormy night. (Leslie Rule)

shining figure. Made of brilliant white light, it stood about nine feet tall. Beth stared, fascinated, wondering why such a bright light did not hurt her eyes.

The light was so dazzling it was impossible to make out anything other than its outline. It had the distinctive form of an angel with wings rising above the shoulders.

Are you an angel?

Beth's question never reached her lips. Her words were unspoken, and yet she heard an answer.

Yes.

The telepathic communication was brief and reassuring. As Beth watched, the figure dissolved.

Suddenly, her worries were gone. She slept peacefully for the rest of the night. Lava Kitty, too, seemed to have gotten a good rest and made it through the night without getting wet.

Beth has told few people about the angelic encounter, and though she was thrilled with the experience, she is not sure why the angel appeared at that moment, though she suspects it was because she was troubled. She had been so worried about the cat she had had an uneasy rest until the being of light appeared.

The next story tells of yet another bedside encounter. The presence of angels soothed a mother's worried mind and, perhaps, healed an ailing boy.

Watching over Them

On a fall night in 2002, Janis Maltos fell asleep in her king-sized bed. "My husband worked nights, so I was alone," said the Fairbanks, Alaska, teacher and mother of two sons. "Later, my three-year-old son, Jared, crawled into my bed. I rubbed his back and said the same prayer I said every night. 'Dear God, bless my son and keep him free of all evil.'"

Janis was worried about Jared. The little boy had some medical problems and also suffered from night terrors. She often awoke to the sound of his screams in the night. In addition, he had been sleepwalking.

Janis Maltos has seen the angels who watch over her family. (Leslie Rule)

"Keep him safe and guarded by your best guardian angels," Janis prayed.

Soon she and Jared drifted off to sleep. A short while later, she was awakened by a bright light. She was astonished to see a small angel, standing on the bed, near her son's feet. Jared had kicked off the blankets, and the angel gazed at him as he slept.

"The angel was a cherub with wings," said Janis. "He was smiling at my son."

She could not believe that what she was seeing was real. "I closed my eyes and opened them again to make sure that I wasn't dreaming."

The little angel looked like a baby, about nine months old. His entire body, even his thick, curly hair, was a translucent white. Janis became aware of a bright light beside the bed. "I looked at the light. It was shaped like a large, faceless angel with wings."

The baby angel seemed to become aware that Janis was watching. "He turned his head toward me," she said. The instant he saw the sleepy woman staring at him, the small angel darted toward the larger figure. "They both disappeared in a bright flash of white light," said Janis.

She was in awe. "I felt no fear," she confided. "I felt comfort, peace and unconditional love."

Janis's worries instantly vanished. Angels were watching over them. Everything would be okay.

Jared soon outgrew the night terrors, and as of this writing, he is a healthy eleven-year-old who earns straight A's.

The day I saw the angel appear beside my bed, I told a friend who responded by sending me a copy of *A Book of Angels,* by Sophy Burnham. Brilliantly written, informative, and filled with uplifting stories, the book captivated me. I was surprised to learn that angel encounters are often preceded by a sheet snapping from the corner of the bed. The author suggested that this was the angels' way of waking people.

I suddenly saw my surroundings from a fresh perspective. I lived in a world with angels! Not only had I seen one, but according to Sophy Burnham's book, many sane and credible people had encountered angels.

As I read, I realized that my twilight angel might have been my second sighting. The book told of the various ways angels manifest themselves. I learned that they sometimes appear in trees and that they are also known to sing.

About a year before the angel appeared in my room, I had seen something in my neighborhood that I found odd, but it did not occur to me that it was a supernatural event until I read Sophy Burnham's book.

One overcast afternoon I had been walking down Madrona Street, a block from my home, when I heard a powerful male voice singing a long, drawn-out note. It was soon followed by words that I didn't understand, but I assumed that they were the lyrics to an Italian opera.

The talented singer was in a tree in the middle of a small front yard. The tree was deciduous, about fifteen feet tall, and the man appeared to be standing in the upper branches. His head and shoulders rose above the leaves, and his lower body was hidden from view. I noted that he was wearing a white shirt and that he was middle aged with thick, curly, black hair.

Though he was facing in my direction and a short distance away, he seemed unaware of me. I walked slowly and sideways for a moment, staring and hoping that he would make eye contact as I tried to make sense of the picture. But the "man" ignored my obvious attempt to connect with him.

I quickly concluded that he must have been pruning branches and had suddenly become inspired to sing. I did not give it another thought until I began to read about angels. I remembered then that the day had been unnaturally still before the singing began. There had been no sound of dogs barking, chattering birds, or car doors slamming. It had been so quiet that the sudden song was all the more startling. The singing abruptly stopped as I walked away.

I had been in a hurry to wrap the peculiar incident in logic. I knew very little about the Italian language, opera, or pruning trees. I didn't recognize any Italian words but hastily decided the man was Italian. I've since realized that people prune from *below* branches, not from above, but I did not take that into consideration when I saw the figure in the treetop.

Could he have been an eccentric man with an amazing voice who climbed a tree on a gray day to serenade the rare passerby?

Perhaps, but I hope he was an angel.

As I continued to read about angels, I learned that it is not unusual for them to sing and that when they do, it is often in a language that listeners do not understand.

Music in itself is something of a miracle. It has the ability to stir our hearts and buoy our spirits. It makes sense that angels use music to communicate.

My literary agent, Sheree Bykofsky, once met a musical angel. I asked her to describe her experience. Here is what she wrote:

In graduate school at Columbia, living in Manhattan, the world was mine. Yet some petty thing had me troubled that day, and as my mom always said about me, I wear my heart on my sleeve. And so, on that day I was walking through the lower east side, looking down at the sidewalk.

If he had not spoken to me, I probably would have missed seeing the barefoot homeless man sitting on the sidewalk, his back against a brick wall.

Sheree Bykofsky met an angel with a message. (Photo courtesy of Sheree Bykofsky)

He said exactly the words I needed to hear: "If you lose your smile, you lose everything."

He was strumming his guitar as he spoke, and the music was beautiful. As I smiled in grateful response to his wisdom, I noticed with astonishment that there were no strings on his instrument.

That I believe was my first—but not my last—encounter with a real angel. His words have stayed with me all these years, and they have helped me many times in many ways.

My third possible angel encounter came a couple of years after I read Sophy Burnham's book. He in no way resembled the classic image of an angel. He appeared to be an ordinary human, but he had such extraordinary timing I will never forget him.

According to Sophy Burnham, angels are around us at all times, and if we need their help, all we have to do is ask. I loved the idea but was not about to ask them to help me with every little problem. It seemed, somehow, that I should reserve my request for when I was really in need.

Then came a time I was struggling with a painful personal issue. I was so upset that I stopped writing, and I abandoned a project that had brought me joy. Since childhood I had wanted to build a miniature town in my backyard. I had finally broken ground and had dug a hole for a tiny lake, lined it with plastic, and filled it with water from the garden hose. I had piled mounds of dirt around the perimeters to create hillsides for the small houses I planned to find or make.

I had decided that a quarter of an inch would represent one real-life foot. I was eager to visualize how the village would look in my chosen scale, so I constructed a crude model of a house from a cereal box. It was a ten-minute project, involving Scotch tape, and

the result was less than satisfying, but it gave me a sense of how
I should size things.

For two weeks I had had fun playing in the dirt, creating little
winding roads and adding moss to look like grass. But as I wrestled
with my problem, I lost interest in the things that made me happy,
and I set aside the project. I had not worked on it for nearly a week
on the day that I became so overwhelmed with emotion I did not
think I could bear it.

I was sitting on my living room couch, unsure of where to turn.
The despair I felt was so intense, I thought I would break in two.
Then I did what I had never done before. I cried out loud, "Angels,
help me!"

The anguished words had barely drifted from my lips when the
doorbell rang. We rarely had company because my (now ex) husband
was a loner who preferred solitude. I opened the door to see a small,
smiling man with dark skin and black hair. His brown eyes held mine,
glittering mischievously, as if we shared a secret joke. He held up two
miniature Victorian style houses. They were made from balsa wood
and were the exact scale I had chosen for my miniature town.

He was selling them for twenty-five dollars apiece. They were
overpriced, but I did not question it. I got the cash from my purse
and bought one of the little houses.

My despair instantly vanished, replaced by a surge of peace and
hope. I knew that the angels had heard me. And I was certain that my
problem would be solved and that everything would be okay.

With a renewed joy, I went straight to the backyard and set the
tiny house on one of the hills that overlooked my little lake. The
house wasn't weatherproof, but it was so much fun to see it there.
And I was inspired to go back to work on the project. I spent the rest
of the day working on the town and marveling at the magic thing
that had occurred.

Was it an angel at my door?

Looking back, I sometimes wish I had watched him from the window to see what he would do next. If he was an angel, he might have disappeared. But at the time of the encounter, my heart was filled with such peace that I did not need answers. I was simply grateful.

I can not say for certain that my visitor was an angel, but he showed up at the precise moment I asked the angels for help. Whoever he was, he rang my doorbell despite the fact I had posted a sign in big, angry red letters that read, ABSOLUTELY NO SOLICITORS! DO NOT KNOCK! DO NOT RING THE DOORBELL!

I worked at a desk near the door and had been interrupted by salesmen several times while writing magazine articles and had lost my concentration. I had posted the sign a few years before, and it had apparently discouraged solicitors because, until now, not one had rung the doorbell.

The problem that had troubled me was soon resolved. In retrospect, the issue itself was not that dreadful. It was my response to the situation that was the real problem. I had worked myself up to the point that I was overcome by emotions so painful that I could not handle them.

And that is why I called out to the angels for help. I just wanted to stop hurting. Not only did the pain go away, but I was instantly transferred to a place of joy and wonder.

Though angels often intervene to save lives, it is also common for them to offer reassurance during times of stress. Sometimes their presence warms us with a feeling of calm, and sometimes they actually help us with our problems.

The following case is an example of angelic assistance that took a most unusual form.

Let There Be Light

When Jon Arno was a boy, his life was in constant upheaval. His parents were missionaries, and the family moved often.

Just as he got settled in a new school and began to make friends, it was time to move again. The Arno family traveled often, preaching the word of God and helping those in need.

Time after time, Jon found himself awkwardly standing in front of a classroom of strangers as a teacher introduced the new kid. It was always an embarrassing moment, especially as he grew into a teen. "I was desperate to fit in," he confided.

When the Arno family moved to the small town of Chattahoochee, Florida, in 1970, Jon felt he had finally found his home. His new friends recognized his athletic ability, and soon he was pitching for the baseball team. "For the first time I felt like I belonged," he said. "People treated me like I had value."

The fifteen-year-old began dating his first girlfriend, and it seemed everything was going his way.

Then his father announced that, once again, they were pulling up roots. It was time to pack their things for a move to Montgomery, Alabama.

Jon was devastated. "It was so frustrating," he said. "And I rebelled."

But his parents were determined to do God's work in a new place, and Jon had no choice but to go along. He was miserable and spent every spare minute talking long distance to his girlfriend. "I had a collection of silver dollars, and I spent them all, calling her," said Jon.

The months dragged on, and Jon could stand it no longer. "I told my parents I was going back to Chattahoochee. "They said it broke their hearts, but they let me go. My dad reached into his wallet and gave me the last of his money."

Jon hitchhiked back to Chattahoochee.

But things were not as easy as he had imagined. He spent a few nights sleeping under bridges until a good-hearted family offered him their couch and a job. He worked hard, assisting brick masons.

Before long he had saved enough money to rent a rundown apartment. It overlooked the Chatta Burger, the fast-food restaurant where all his friends hung out. Jon was thrilled. "I couldn't believe that they would lease an apartment to a sixteen-year-old kid," he said.

On his own for the first time, he had never thought about things like electricity or paying bills and was a little surprised to find that the lights didn't come on with a flick of the switch. "I guess I thought the power came with the apartment," he said with a laugh.

It was springtime, but it had been raining all morning, and the afternoon was gray as Jon walked the two miles to the power company. "The power company was in a small building, and I remember that the clerk was an older, balding man. He told me I was twenty dollars short."

Embarrassed, Jon told the clerk he'd be back later with the cash, though he had no idea where he would get it. He pushed open the glass door and stepped out onto the quiet street. Where would he get the money?

He had been so excited about his first night in the new apartment, but now he was discouraged. "It really troubled me," he confessed.

Without electricity, he would have no hot water for a shower, no way to cook, and would likely spend the evening sitting in the dark. It might be many days before he earned the money for the deposit.

Barely a minute had passed after he left the power company's office when he heard the squeal of tires in the distance. The approaching car was moving so fast that it was nearly upon him as he was about to cross the street.

Startled, Jon stepped back from the curb. "The car came barreling around the corner and was careening all over the road," he remembered. "I thought it must be a drunk driver. He was gunning it."

Suddenly the automobile slammed to a stop and then pulled up beside him. "It was a low rider, and I couldn't see the driver," said Jon, explaining that he stood too high on the curb to see into the window of the "big, two-toned gas guzzler."

A large, masculine hand reached out through the window and held out a twenty-dollar bill. "Here is the money you need," said the stranger.

Jon was dumfounded. "I don't know you. How will I pay you back?" he asked.

"It doesn't matter, Jon. Take it." The voice was low and commanding and had an odd echoing quality.

Stunned, Jon reached for the money. The instant his fingers closed upon the bill, the car lurched forward and zoomed down the road.

The clerk was obviously surprised to see the teen return so quickly, but he didn't ask questions as he accepted the payment and wrote out the receipt. He told Jon that his power would be turned on later that afternoon.

In a daze, Jon walked home. Who in the world was in that car, and how did he know he needed twenty dollars? There had been no one but Jon and the clerk in the utility building. And even if there had been, there was no time for anyone to rush out, get into a car, and drive up to give him the money.

The car had been several blocks away when Jon left the building. He had heard its tires screeching in the distance.

"Less than two minutes passed from the moment the clerk told me I didn't have enough money and the moment I started to cross the street," Jon emphasized, still in awe over the mystery nearly four decades later.

Today Jon is assistant branch director for the Federal Emergency Management Agency in Atlanta, Georgia. He often finds himself contemplating the enigmatic exchange with a stranger who not only knew his name but also knew he needed twenty dollars.

"I knew everyone in town, and I'd never seen that car before. I didn't recognize the voice," he said, adding that the arm was hairy and very large with olive-colored skin. The skin tone was similar to that of the people his family had helped when they were in Brazil.

Had the stranger been an angel?

Jon believes he was. "I eventually met my wife there." They have two grown children and a grandchild. His time in Chattahoochee seemed destined to be. He is grateful to the angel for reminding him that someone is looking after him, and stressed, "God was taking care of me."

Though the angels are always with us, they are selective about their intervention. The aid given to Jon not only solved a small problem, it energized his faith.

A woman facing a serious worry asked God for assistance, and she believes an angel was sent to help her. Here is her story.

Bargain with God

The year 1983 was rough for Nancy Williams. The young Hendersonville, Tennessee, mother suffered a second failed marriage and was overwhelmed with worry.

Her daughter, Brandy, was the center of her life. Nancy doted on the two-year-old and vowed to always be there for her. But on a dark November day, she realized that that was not up to her.

An X-ray showed a small black spot on Nancy's right lung.

"I was a heavy smoker," she admitted. "I smoked three packs of cigarettes a day. I was terrified it was cancer."

Nancy was scheduled for a biopsy. At the time of the frightening discovery she had been hospitalized for an unrelated non–life-threatening illness, so she had spent the night before surgery in her hospital room.

"I had lost several people close to me to cancer," she said. She knew how quickly a malignancy could spread. Her sweet toddler was her first concern. If Nancy had lung cancer, Brandy might grow up without a mother.

Who will raise my baby? she worried as hot tears streamed down her cheeks.

Her father was disabled, and her mother was overwhelmed taking care of him. "God, who will take care of Brandy if you take my life away?"

Nancy tried to bargain with God. "Let me live to raise my child," she begged. "And I will never smoke another cigarette."

The door opened and a nurse walked in. "She was short and pudgy," remembered Nancy. The nurse appeared to be in her late thirties and wore her long, light brown hair in the old-fashioned 1960s style with the flipped-up ends. Her uniform, too, was outdated. But the thing that struck Nancy the most was the compassion in the woman's eyes.

"Honey, are you alright?" asked the nurse.

"No!" Nancy cried.

The nurse carried no chart, but she seemed to know her situation. "You're the one going in for a biopsy in the morning," she said. Her voice was soft and sweet.

"Yes," said Nancy. "I'm not afraid to die. I know I will be with Jesus. But who will take care of my baby?"

As Nancy stared into the woman's eyes, she saw her own fear and pain reflected back. "I could see that it hurt her to see me hurting," she said.

"Would you like me to pray with you?" asked the nurse. "Do you believe Jesus will heal you?"

Nancy nodded and felt warm fingers curl around hers. "As soon as she took my hand, I felt a calmness—a peace," she said. "I closed my eyes, and a warm tingling started at the top of my head and emanated through my body."

The words of the prayer are lost to time past, forgotten as the years have gone by. But Nancy will never forget the exhilarating sensation as the kind nurse softly prayed. "At one point I opened my eyes and saw the whitest light shining off of her. It was so bright. There is nothing on this earth to compare it to."

After a few moments, the nurse said, "Go to sleep now, honey. God has taken care of everything."

The doctor did indeed give Nancy good news after the biopsy. The spot on her lung, he said, was a scar from pneumonia.

"I don't remember ever having pneumonia," Nancy told me.

The only thing that mattered was that the doctor had given her a clean bill of health—along with a stern warning. "You were lucky this time," he said. "But next time you might not be. If you want to see your child grow up, you will quit smoking."

Nancy never again touched another cigarette. "I didn't even want one," she said. Her desire for nicotine had miraculously vanished.

"When I was released from the hospital I went to the nurses' station to ask about the nurse who prayed with me," Nancy said.

But the day nurse shook her head. "There's nobody here who fits that description," she insisted. The two nurses who had worked the night shift looked nothing like the woman Nancy had met.

It wasn't possible, she was told, that someone could come in off the street. The doors had been locked for security reasons.

"I know who it was," said Nancy. "It was my guardian angel. I feel very blessed that God loved me enough to send me one of his angels."

As it turned out, God has sent her at least *two* of his angels, for a few months later she met another. She was just beginning her four o'clock waitress shift on a warm summer afternoon at Po Folks restaurant when a raggedy, older man came in. "He looked like a drifter," she said, describing his tattered clothing and long, scraggly gray hair.

Nancy and Norma, the other waitress, were a little bit nervous as they eyed the man. "We were afraid he was there to rob us," she admitted.

But the stranger settled into a booth. As Nancy approached, he looked up and said, "How are you, Nancy?"

She was startled to hear him call her by name. She did not recognize him and was not wearing a name tag, yet he seemed to know her. He told her that he had come to the restaurant because he was waiting for his car to be repaired.

This struck her as a little strange, for the closest mechanic's shop was at least a mile away. There were plenty of other restaurants that were closer, and she wondered why he hadn't chosen to wait in one of them.

"I'd like a cup of coffee," said the man. "And I'd like to have me a piece of blackberry cobbler with ice cream. But I don't have any money."

"Sir, I don't have any money either," said Nancy. "I just started my shift, and I've been off work for a few days."

He opened a briefcase, and Nancy noticed a watercolor paint set inside. Then he pulled out small cardboard paintings and showed them to her. The images depicted Bible scenes with Scriptures. They were sweet little pictures but certainly not great works of art.

"He told me that he was selling them for a dollar and a quarter a piece. He asked me to see if any of the restaurant employees would buy them."

Nancy obliged and showed the paintings to the manager and the cooks, but as she expected, everyone just shook their heads. They had no use for the simple paintings.

She was not about to let the man go hungry. Nancy borrowed four dollars from Norma and bought him desert and coffee.

He ate gratefully, and as he did so, he asked her, "Do you still go to Cornerstone Church in Gallitan?"

"Why, yes, I do." Nancy searched her mind but could not remember ever meeting this man. "How did you know what church I go to?" she asked.

The man smiled but would not answer her question. "All I want to say is that you should keep walking the path you are on. You are a fine, upstanding young lady. You will go far."

As he got up to leave he said, "I don't have money for a tip, so I'd like to leave you these." He handed her four of his little paintings.

Nancy thanked him, and she and Norma watched as he went out the door. Big windows flanked the front entrance, so they expected to see him walking past one of the windows. But there was no movement in the windows. Nancy felt a slow chill creep up her neck.

"Where did he go?" asked Norma.

The women were baffled. Nancy ran to a booth and slid in close to the window, peering out. "I don't see him!" she exclaimed.

Norma raced to the kitchen and went out the back door.

"I ran out the front door," said Nancy. "We circled the restaurant, but he had just disappeared!"

The restaurant sat in the middle of a shopping mall's huge parking lot. There were no other buildings nearby—nowhere the man could have hidden. It was before the dinner rush, and business was slow that time of day. The parking lot was nearly empty. The women searched, but the man had not ducked behind a car.

"I couldn't wait to tell Daddy," said Nancy. Her father was very religious. He listened thoughtfully to her story and then nodded his head. He believed that she had definitely had a spiritual encounter. "Your faith was tested today," he told her. "You passed the test."

Thoughts of angels bring comfort to people of many faiths from around the globe. This statue strikes a powerful pose on the verdant grounds of The National Sanctuary of our Sorrowful Mother (also known as The Grotto) in Portland, Oregon. (Leslie Rule)

Angels Among Us in the News

ANGELS AROUND

A BLOWING ROCK, NORTH CAROLINA, chiropractor told a reporter, "There are angels around," when he narrowly escaped serious injury and perhaps death in December 2010.

Dr. Walter Holloway, sixty-nine, was driving his Toyota SUV down West View Drive near his home when the vehicle slid toward the edge of a sheer cliff and rolled onto its side, where it was stopped from plunging to Highway 321 below by a few frail branches and a thin tree.

Rescuers from the Blowing Rock Fire Department could hardly believe it when they found that the two-ton SUV was supported only by a spindly tree, not much thicker than a man's leg. Fearing that the tree could suddenly snap, the crew worked quickly. They used cables and winches to secure the vehicle before helping the doctor to safety via a high-angle ladder truck with an attached bucket.

Rescuers were surprised not only by the fact that a slender tree had stopped the SUV but by the miracle that anyone had noticed Dr. Holloway's predicament. The car was somewhat hidden by brush, and few people traveling the road below bothered to glance up. But an observant nine-year-old, Adam Patterson of Jamestown, North Carolina, noticed the precariously balanced SUV and told his father, who called 9-1-1.

Dr. Holloway, a devout Baptist who survived without a scratch, was not shy about giving credit to God's angels for saving his life. (Sources include WBTV.)

NOT HIS TIME

A FAYETTEVILLE, NORTH CAROLINA, teenager was struck by a train and insisted that his life was spared by an angel who came to his aid. The nineteen-year-old was dressed in a Victorian costume and headed downtown toward Fayetteville's annual celebration, "A Dickens Festival," on Friday afternoon, November 23, 2007. He stood on the train tracks, near Hay Street, waiting for a southbound train to pass on adjacent tracks. The tremendous roar of the first train's engine blended in with the noise of a northbound train as it barreled toward him.

Horrified passersby shouted warnings as they saw the approaching train and the oblivious boy in its path, but their shrieks were drowned out by the sound of the trains.

The panicked conductor blew the whistle and braked but was pulling a string of ninety-three cars and was unable to avoid hitting the teen, though he did manage to slow the train's speed to twenty miles per hour.

The impact resulted in injuries that included fractured ribs, a broken arm, and a leg so badly damaged that it required above-the-knee amputation. The boy, however, escaped with his life and credited an angel who appeared as he lay beneath the moving train and pinned him down, preventing further injury.

The teenager told reporters that the angel had told him, "It wasn't my time."

His mother pronounced his survival "a miracle," adding that it strengthened her faith in God. (Sources include WRAL TV and *The Fayetteville Observer.*)

ANGELS AWAITING

A DYING TEN-YEAR-OLD Clermont, Ohio, boy was the only one who could see the angels around him—until they were captured in photographs. Ryan Reynolds had an inoperable brain tumor and had been seeing angels his entire life. Sometimes his mother, Shirley Reynolds, overheard his side of the conversation as he talked to them.

Ryan died in mid-April 2003, and his mother later shared his story with WCPO TV in Cincinnati. She told a reporter that two months before Ryan's death, they had gone on a picnic and during a hayride, her son had told her he could see his angel.

Shirley Reynolds took pictures that day and was surprised to find inexplicable milky-white images among the people in the prints. When she showed Ryan the transparent shapes, he said, "That's my angel, Mommy. She talks to me all the time."

Shirley would have dismissed the anomalies as defects caused by the film developing process, but two professional photographers who took pictures during the picnic found that their shots also contained the mysterious images.

Though not distinctly angel shaped, the images could not be scientifically explained. They appeared as speckles, globes, and a "fish-shaped" object. The professional photographers agreed that the transparent shapes were not reflections or dust or water on the lens and that their appearance in the photographs was unlike anything they'd seen before.

ANGELS AMONG THE STARS

ANGELS APPEAR to all types of people, including celebrities. A few stars have come forward over the years to publicly share the details of their encounters.

Academy Award–winning actor Denzel Washington was quoted in various publications a few years back when he mentioned a childhood sighting of an angel. The angel, he said, looked a lot like his sister, Lorice, but she had wings. When Denzel opened the door to let more light into the room so he could get a better look, the angel faded away. His mother told him it was his guardian angel.

Country music star Sammy Kershaw told reporters from both *Country Weekly* and *The Boot* that an angel saved his life in 1980 when he lived in Oklahoma. Depressed, newly divorced, and struggling with his music career, he had decided to end his life. As he prepared to shoot himself in the boiler room of his dry cleaning business, he heard someone come into the store.

He had never met the older woman who told him she had come by to check on him. They chatted for a few minutes, and when she left, he followed her outside only to find that she had vanished. He knew God had sent an angel and never again considered suicide.

Chapter Seven

THE IMPOSSIBLE

FEW PEOPLE REALIZE THE
PROFOUND PART ANGELIC FORCES PLAY
IN HUMAN EVENTS.

—*Billy Graham,* FAMOUS EVANGELIST AND AUTHOR OF
Angels: God's Secret Agents

When it comes to angels, the impossible becomes possible.

In the winter of 2010, a Haitian earthquake victim lived twenty-seven days without water. Authorities said it was impossible.

The twenty-eight-year-old man survived nearly a month pinned beneath rubble in the aftermath of the January 12, 2010, magnitude 7.0 earthquake. Officials said he must have found access to water. No one, they said, could survive that long without it.

Evan Monsigrace insisted that he *did* have water, occasionally brought to him by a man in a white coat. His story was dismissed as a hallucination. Although he was disoriented after the traumatic episode and may very well have been hallucinating, there is still no earthly explanation as to how he got water.

Evan sold rice in a marketplace and was trapped on his side beneath the collapsed structure. His mother confirmed that he had indeed been missing since the day of the quake that claimed over two hundred thousand lives.

Authorities combed the devastation and believed that they had found the last of the survivors as Evan waited in the darkness. All rescue efforts had ceased two weeks before a cleanup crew discovered him as they were bulldozing the ruins.

The fact that Evan Monsigrace was found and not crushed by the bulldozers is a miracle in itself. He was emaciated and dehydrated, with open sores on his hands and feet, but was otherwise fine.

If the mysterious "man" in white who occasionally brought him water was a human being, he would have had to dig through mounds of debris to reach Evan and then cover him again in rubble. It is an unlikely scenario.

Experts say that humans deprived of liquids usually die from dehydration within three to seven days but that the humidity could have extended Evan's life for up to five extra days. The doctors who treated the earthquake survivor were flabbergasted by the fact he had survived for four weeks. His normal kidney function indicated that he must have had some fluids.

Doctors and reporters grasped for a logical explanation for the man's survival. They suggested that maybe he had found some of the fruit sold at the market by other vendors.

Maybe. But he was pinned to the ground by concrete and could not reach far. If a piece of fruit did roll within his reach, how did it sustain him for so many days? And why does he remember a man in white giving him water?

Certainly there could be a "logical" reason for Evan's survival. But after finding so many irrefutable accounts of angelic intervention, my guess is that this is another example of supernatural forces at work.

When such an extraordinary thing occurs, public officials rarely credit angels. Perhaps they suspect divine intervention but are too embarrassed to admit it.

I can't say that I blame them. Despite the fact that so many of us believe in angels, most of us would balk if reporters and authorities automatically credited the angels whenever someone miraculously survived.

It's not every day that the impossible becomes possible. That is why it is so hard for us to accept it. A friend of mine saw something peculiar a few years back, and she still can't accept it. She knows what she witnessed, but she also knows that it was "impossible."

Tracie and her friend Michelle were strolling on a wooded trail on a summer afternoon with their children. Tracie's younger son, three-year-old Scott, suddenly broke into a run. He tripped, and Tracie watched, horrified, as he sailed toward a sharp stick that protruded from the ground. Soon his eye was inches away from making contact with the pointed end.

But Scott landed safely, a foot or so from the stick. "It didn't make sense within the rules of physics," said Tracie.

It wasn't as if Scott was pulled to one side. He was just suddenly *there*, a safe distance from the stick. Michelle and Tracie's older son, Clayton, also witnessed the incident, and each viewed it from different angles. Everyone said it was an odd sight.

It was as if they had been watching a movie where one scene suddenly cut to another. It was as if a loop of film were snipped from life's movie, with no images of Scott actually moving from point A to point B. It was as if the great director in the sky was snipping out frames of film so that there was no segue from the impending disaster to the happy ending.

As I interview people about their miraculous rescues, I've discovered that this type of thing is not as rare as we might expect.

The lady in the next case is another example. The scene of her journey to safety must have ended up on Heaven's cutting room floor. One moment she was doomed, and in the next she was far from the danger, with no explanation of how she was transported.

Coffee Break with an Angel

When Virginia George looks back on the frightening incident on December 11, 2009, the entire event mystifies her. The eighty-year-old Danbury, Connecticut, resident had been out shopping and was driving from one store to the next when she had a sudden impulse to stop at her house for coffee.

It was, she said, completely out of character. "I normally would finish all my shopping first," Virginia told me. Yet she was strangely compelled to break her routine. It was a life-saving decision.

Virginia parked her car in the garage of the home she had had built in the 1960s and now shared with her sister, Gerri, and walked to her kitchen.

When she heard the explosion, she assumed that her furnace had blown up.

It did not occur to her that her *car* had exploded. The force of the blast had destroyed the car and ripped chunks out of the concrete garage floor. If she had not changed her plans, Virginia would have been in the driver's seat in the middle of traffic when the car blew up.

She did not realize that her car was on fire and that flames were spreading from the attached garage toward the house. She smelled smoke and knew she should evacuate but figured there was plenty of time to warn her nephew in his downstairs apartment and get her pocketbook.

She pounded on her nephew's door, and he and his friends escaped into the yard through his apartment's outside door. By the time she had walked back upstairs and found her purse, smoke was swirling around her, and it was becoming difficult to breathe.

Virginia headed toward the back door. "I needed to get through two doors to get outside," she said, explaining that one was a hallway door and the other was the locked door on her back porch. The doors were lined up, about four feet from each other, and both were closed.

She was a little panicked and hoped she could stay alert long enough to make it outside before she was overcome by the thickening smoke. Suddenly, she felt pressure on her back. "Someone pushed me!" she exclaimed.

In the next instant, she found herself outside, face down in a snow bank, ten feet from the back door. Virginia stood up and brushed herself off.

How had she gotten there?

"The last thing I remember is being pushed," she confided. "I don't know who unlocked the door."

She had no memory of being transported through two closed doors and thrown into the yard. She was uninjured but distraught. Her house was burning!

A TV news crew and the fire department arrived simultaneously. "It was the coldest day of the year," said Virginia. "The fire hydrants were frozen."

She watched helplessly as her home went up in flames. It was devastating, yet she knew she had much to be thankful for. "It's a miracle my sister wasn't home," she said. Gerri had been babysitting their great-niece and was late getting home because the child's mother had been delayed.

While the timing was a blessing, Virginia's escape from the fire was a miracle.

Who or what had pushed her out the doors?

I consulted a seasoned firefighter, asking if it were possible that the chemical components of the blaze could have created a pressure strong enough to push a person out the doors. When I described the situation, I was told that it was impossible.

An inferno can indeed blow people out of doors, he told me, but they are badly burned. Even firefighters, dressed in protective gear, are burned when blown from burning structures.

In addition, when Virginia was shoved out the doors, her house was filled with deadly smoke, but the environment did not yet contain the kind of pressure to expel her.

The sisters lost their home and Virginia's car. While insurance covered the house, it did not cover her car. The fire had originated in the automobile, caused by an undetermined mechanical problem.

Most people are retired by age eighty, but Virginia not only works in the city's planning and zoning department, she also has a job as a receptionist at a healthcare facility.

The community rallied around the lifelong residents, taking up a collection to help with expenses. Virginia was thrilled when car dealership owners Raymond and David Beylouni donated a silver 2002 Chevy Cavalier so she could commute to work.

She was overwhelmed by the generosity of both friends and strangers who came to her aid. "I am grateful to everyone," she said. And she is also thankful to someone else: the angel who shoved her to safety.

Virginia has attended daily mass for many years and has always believed that God's angels watch over her. She will never forget the moment that two strong hands pushed her with such power that she flew twenty feet yet landed so softly that she wasn't even bruised.

The woman in the following story shares common ground with Virginia. She, too, had a roommate named Gerri, came close to losing her life in a fire, and escaped in a most unusual way.

Out of the Ashes

Susan Cohen woke to the sound of her roommate's shrieks. She lifted her head from her pillow. It was 3:30 A.M. on March 6, 1973, in Silver Springs, Maryland.

Susan and her roommate, Gerri, shared a seventh-floor apartment in the Georgian Towers, a complex of high-rise brick buildings that covered four square blocks.

Gerri sounded scared, her voice carrying from her room down the hall. "Fire!"

Susan got out of bed. "I didn't realize the fire was in *our* apartment," she told me. "I figured it was somewhere else in the building, so I opened my bedroom door. I was hit with a blast of smoke and heat."

The fire was in 716D, the two-bedroom unit the young women shared.

Before going to bed, Gerri had left a cigarette burning in an ashtray atop an antique end table in the living room. While the women slept, the cigarette burned down and toppled over onto the table, where it had smoldered for hours. The spot of red embers grew into a raging blaze, with heat so intense that the kitchen telephone melted.

Now, Susan had unwittingly opened her door. Smoke poured from the hallway into her room. Terrified, she ran to her bedroom window. "Smoke was billowing all around me," she remembered. "I slid open the window and yelled for help."

Gerri climbed from her window and stepped out onto a narrow ledge. The screams of the two women began to rouse residents.

Soon a crowd of people gathered below, and they shouted encouragement. "Hold on! Help is coming! The fire truck is on its way!"

"I could hardly breathe," said Susan. Dense, dark smoke filled the room and burned her lungs. She swung a leg out the window, straddling the sill. "I was half hanging out," she said.

The living room balcony was just inches from her window. Susan would have climbed onto it, but the heat had shattered the glass doors, and the fire had spread to the balcony furniture. There was nowhere to turn.

"I knew that the carpet could catch fire any second," she told me. "I would have to make a choice: Jump or burn to death."

Seven floors below, the concerned crowd continued to shout. "Hold on!"

What was taking so long?

Susan did not know that the firefighters had been accidentally directed to the wrong building. As she and Gerri tried to stay alive, the firefighters were dragging hoses up seven flights of stairs in a building on the opposite side of the complex.

"No one showed up to help," said Susan. "It seemed to be taking an eternity. I thought my life was over."

Just when she was certain she could not bear another second, someone was suddenly beside her in her bedroom.

Oh my God! Someone is here! she thought, sweet relief flowing over her as her rescuer wrapped her face in a wet towel. She was led through the burning apartment, out into the corridor, and down the many stairs. She was dumb with shock as they crossed the parking lot to the complex lobby.

Susan's rescuer deposited her on the sofa and told her everything would be okay. "I was suddenly alone," she said. "You would think that whoever saved me would have stayed with me, but they left without saying good-bye." She did not see them go.

"A little while later, I saw the firefighters come in with my roommate on a gurney. Then I heard a firefighter shouting, 'We can't find the roommate.'"

Susan knew that he meant her. "They thought I was dead," she explained. "I told them, 'I'm right here!'"

"How did you get out?" he demanded.

"One of your men came in and got me out," she replied.

"That's impossible!" said the stunned fireman. "The door to your apartment is metal and too hot to touch. We had to break the door down with an axe."

Susan and Gerri were treated for smoke inhalation but were otherwise fine. They learned that as they screamed for their lives, their apartment had become a virtual inferno. The clothing in their closet melted on the hangers, and the cans of food in their kitchen cupboards exploded. It should have been impossible for a human being to walk through the burning apartment without protective gear. Yet Susan had.

Today, she is the mother of a grown son and works at a Washington, D.C., law firm. "I assumed it was a fireman who got me out of there," she said. She hadn't been able to see much with the towel over her face. The low, reassuring voice of her rescuer could have belonged to either a man or a woman.

"I called my mom the day after the fire to tell her what happened," said Susan. "Before I could say anything, she blurted out that she had a weird dream about my grandmother."

Her grandmother had died years before, and Susan had inherited a pair of lovely antique end tables—the very tables that had flanked the sofa in the destroyed apartment. The fire, in fact, was sparked by the cigarette carelessly left burning in an ashtray on one of those tables.

In her mother's dream, the grandmother had appeared and fretted, "Something terrible is happening to my end tables!"

The end tables, of course, were now nothing but ashes.

"It may have been my grandmother who saved me from the fire. Or maybe it was an angel sent by her," she ventured. "I know that people's lives have been affected because I'm here," she told me, describing how she had started a speed dating service that led to thirty marriages.

Susan recognizes the fact that when her life was spared, it gave her a chance to help others. She takes pride in the knowledge that her dating service not only resulted in many happy marriages but led to the births of dozens of children.

Was that the reason for her miraculous survival?

No one can say, of course, but it is something to consider. If the mysterious rescuer had arrived a moment later, it would have been too late for Susan. And our Earth would be minus many children—children who could be destined to do wonderful things.

When Susan heard the details of the fire's devastation, she shuddered. How was it possible she had walked through the burning apartment?

I was most curious about the hot metal door and asked her, "Did your rescuer shut the door once you made it to the corridor?"

Susan paused and then said slowly, "You are going to think I'm crazy, but I think we went *through* the closed door."

I do not think she is crazy, but I find it very interesting that both Susan Cohen and Virginia George escaped deadly fires via closed doors.

And both women are certain they were saved by divine intervention.

People moving through closed doors? It's a tough concept to embrace. But the more people I interview about angelic intervention, the more I believe that angels can ignore the laws of physics, twisting the rules for those they assist.

They also seem to have an unusual way of speaking with people. They frequently use telepathy, projecting images or words directly into the minds of human beings.

I was admittedly a little skeptical when people first began to confide in me about their telepathic communication with angels. Though I tried to keep an open mind, I couldn't help but wonder if their experiences were simply imagination.

If the images and voices are within people's minds, how could they be sure that they weren't simply thoughts conjured up by their own brains?

I noted, however, that their descriptions of the encounters were very similar. Again and again, sane people told me that though the voices were not heard through their ears, they were not thoughts. They *knew* that the words that imprinted upon their minds came from an outside source. In most cases, they had never experienced such a thing before and have not experienced it since.

The voices were so clear that some folks could not determine whether they had heard them with their ears or within their heads. The "voices" were very real, they told me. I asked a lot of questions and could sense some people getting frustrated when I didn't understand. But I've talked to enough subjects that now I do understand.

Throughout the pages of this book I've included many cases of people who actually saw or heard angels. Unless I have indicated otherwise, the angels were seen with their eyes or heard with their ears. I've avoided using cases of angels sensed telepathically. But so many people have told me about the phenomenon that I feel obliged to mention it.

The stories I include in my books cover experiences by sane, sober, and honest people. They are not prone to hallucinations, and their spirit encounters are isolated incidents.

Over the last months, as I gathered angel experiences, I sometimes talked to people while on the run and did not have time to immediately interview them about their encounters, so I took their phone numbers and told them I would call.

Coincidentally, I made two phone calls in a row to two women who did not know each other, but each described the same thing. Initially, each had told me that, yes, they had seen angels. But months later, when I worked my way through piles of research material and finally got around to calling them, each one warned me that her story might not be what I was looking for.

While they did "see" angels, it was not with their eyes. The visions were within their minds but so vivid they knew it was not imagination. If I had spoken to only one of these women, I probably would not have included her experience in this book. But the fact that the two women were consistent in their descriptions indicates that their angel visits were real. And if they experienced angels telepathically, then many of my readers probably have too and will want to know more about this type of angel communication.

Both women "saw" angels in their mind's eye. In each incident, the angels were giants. And both women had their experience while under duress, though their circumstances were different. Each sighting brought a surge of tranquility.

Keitha Crane, a Puyallup, Washington, antique dealer, rescued a friend from an abusive relationship. Her friend had been beaten, so Keitha invited her to stay in her home. But the abuser showed up at the house, flashing a gun.

He finally left, but Keitha was so shaken, she could not sleep that night. Her terror cut through her being, and at one point, as she lay in bed, she could not turn her head for fear that she would see the evil man standing there.

She prayed for help, and that is when she saw the angels. "They were on the roof," she told me. "There were lots of them, and they were giants in armor." The angels were obviously protecting her, and she felt instant calm.

Though she was inside the house, she was able to "see" the roof full of angels telepathically.

Janet Fagan, a Seattle artist and teacher, was distressed about a relationship. The burden of her emotions weighed on her as she got off a bus and took her usual shortcut through an old cemetery. She had a decision to make, but she did not know what to do. "I saw two giant angels," she told me.

She could "see" them from the corners of her eyes. The brilliant beings towered over her, and she felt their protective influence. Her anxiety disintegrated, replaced by a sense of peace.

Neither Keitha nor Janet was aware that angels often appear as giants, yet they each "saw" their protectors as towering beings.

In the next story, a woman received telepathic reassurance from beyond during the most terrifying instant of her life.

A Voice in the Dark

It was December 1990 and the Enumclaw, Washington, mother of three young children was driving home from a Christmas party. "I worked in the claims department for Mutual of Enumclaw insurance," Carole Coxen told me. "I was newly divorced and depressed and not paying much attention. It was a dark, drizzly night, and I was going forty-five miles an hour down Highway 169."

She was lost in thought when the pickup truck in front of her stopped suddenly.

"I didn't notice until it was too late," she said. "I slammed on my brakes, but they failed!"

Her little Toyota Corolla crashed into the back of the Ford pickup truck. "Time seemed to stop," she confided. "It was as if everything was moving in slow motion."

With a rush of horror, she thought, *Oh my God! I'm going to die! Who is going to take care of my kids?*

In that split second of panic, she heard a voice.

"You are not going to die. You will be hurt, but you will be okay."

Though she "heard" the reassuring words, it was not with her ears. The voice came from within, as if someone were communicating telepathically.

The car was totaled. And as the mysterious voice had told her, Carole *was* hurt. She suffered a lost tooth and two black eyes.

"The paramedics looked at the smashed car and were stunned," she said. "They couldn't believe I'd survived!"

But she had. Her car was crumpled like an aluminum can, but Carole walked away with life and limbs intact. Two weeks later she was well enough to go back to work.

Carole is grateful she escaped with minor injuries, and she wonders whether the presence who spoke to her may have had something to do with that. At the very least, it soothed her. "The voice was authoritative, and it calmed me in a moment of hysteria," said Carole. "I believe it was an angel, sent by God."

While many report that angels have reassured them during times of stress, it is even more incredible when they intervene to spare our lives.

Read on to the next chapter for more accounts of angelic rescue.

Chapter Eight
ANGELS
ON THE ROAD

WE LOOK BACK WITH SHAME AT THE TIMES
WHEN WE THOUGHT OUR ANGELS HAD
DESERTED US. WITH HINDSIGHT, WE SEE THAT
WE WERE NOT BEING SHUNNED, BUT SAVED
AND BLESSED FOR A MUCH MORE
PRODUCTIVE FUTURE.

—*Brad and Sherry Steiger,*
PROLIFIC COAUTHORS OF BOOKS ON THE MYSTICAL

It seems that angels have been especially busy since the invention
of the wheel. Fragile human bodies weren't designed to move at the
speeds that wheels allow.

Wagons and bicycles and cars and motorcycles, however, are a
great convenience, and I doubt that people will ever give them up.

While we propel ourselves forward at unnatural speeds, our angels are riding along, right beside us.

A few years back some friends of mine were in a tragic accident that took one life. The family mourned for him but was so grateful that the life of their young daughter was spared. After the accident, the little girl reported that "there was someone in the car with us." That someone had pressed against her, holding her against the seat when the car crashed. She was not wearing her seat belt, and if not for the mysterious presence, she might not have survived.

It is an odd thing to be both grateful and grieving at the same time. In this type of situation, people wonder why everyone couldn't be saved.

"Why was I spared when my friend died?" a woman saved by an angel asked me.

"That is a question that people have been asking forever," I told her. "And we won't know the answer until we are on the other side."

If we believe that there is life after death (and I do), then no one is really lost. Still, when we come close to losing life, it becomes more precious. Many who have been rescued by angels have told me that they now live more joyously.

I've spoken with a number of people who believe that they are here because of angelic intervention. While collecting angel stories for this book, I quickly discovered that the most common cases involved dangerous situations on the road. While sometimes the angels appeared during a collision; other times they manifested themselves afterward to reassure frightened accident victims.

In the case of my friend Lelabelle Wolfert, an angel actually helped with the driving. Lelabelle is an Albuquerque, New Mexico, author, and she told me of her arduous automobile trip across the country in the 1930s. She was only five years old when she and her mother and fourteen-year-old sister traveled to California to see relatives.

When her exhausted mother dozed off while driving, her teenage sister tearfully grabbed the wheel and steered them off the road. Soon after, they pulled into a diner, where a man approached them, introducing himself as Gabe.

The stranger told them that he had lost his family in a disaster and needed a ride to San Francisco, their destination.

Lelabelle's mother noted that he had the cleanest hands she'd ever seen and decided he was harmless. The trip went smoothly after that, with Gabe sharing the driving and even changing a flat tire.

"My sister asked him if Gabe was short for Gabriel," remembers Lelabelle. "He smiled and said it was."

When they reached San Francisco, Gabe insisted on being dropped off on the side of the road. "He got out of the car," said Lelabelle. "My mother wanted to say good-bye to him, but first she leaned over the seat to get her purse out of the backseat. When she got out of the car he was nowhere in sight. He just disappeared."

No human could have vanished so quickly. Bewildered, they sat in the car and contemplated the odd occurrence. They suddenly realized the significance of his name. *Gabriel.* They knew then that they had met an angel.

While Lelabelle and her family had clearly seen their angel, Maureen Reintjes, of Merriam, Kansas, did not so much as glimpse hers.

She was driving to work in her SUV one winter morning when a car in the oncoming lane hit black ice. She watched in horror as the car slid sideways into her path. Before she could react, she too was sliding over the invisible ice.

"The next thing I knew, my SUV started to roll over," she told me.

"Lord, protect me," she prayed.

Her vehicle rolled over four times before landing on its passenger side in a field. Maureen, still strapped into her seat, checked herself for injuries. She was shaken but unharmed. "I wondered how I was going to undo my seat belt without falling down to the passenger door," she said.

But almost instantly a rescuer in uniform was there. "I thought that maybe I had blacked out and lost track of time, but it turned out that he just happened to be driving behind me!"

The man was the fire chief from a nearby town, and he seemed shocked that Maureen had survived. "He thought I'd be dead," she said. "The crash was so violent that a Bic pen was stuck in the windshield. Not an area of the car wasn't crushed, but right over my head the roof was bashed upward instead of inward. The back windshield, instead of crunching outward, was crushed in, and it looked like something had flown into the car."

As he helped Maureen out of the vehicle, the chief asked about the passenger. When she told him that she was alone, he didn't believe her. "He kept asking about the other person, and I kept telling him there was no other person."

The chief insisted, "Yes, there was. I saw him."

Maureen did not doubt him. For she, too, had sensed someone else in the car. "Right after I asked God to protect me, I felt something hold me into my seat," she said. "It wasn't my seat belt. It was as if someone was sitting behind me and wrapped their arms around me."

Like Maureen, the woman in the next story found herself arguing with a rescuer about who was on the scene.

A Hand to Hold

It was about eight o'clock on a cool morning on October 1, 1998.
Deborah Treadway, forty-three, drove south along Route 40 in the
town of North East, Maryland. "I was on my way to work," she told
me. "I was in the fast lane, and there was a tractor trailer in the slow
lane."

The tractor trailer hid Deborah's blue Dodge Neon from the
view of a driver approaching the intersection. The man was driving
along Red Toad Road and in a hurry to get to work. He saw only
the tractor trailer as he shot across the road, straight into Deborah's
path.

There was no time to avoid a crash.

Deborah found herself trapped in her crunched car. "I had
slumped down in the seat and was beneath the dashboard," she said.
"The airbags deployed. I didn't know that airbags have dust that flies
out of them."

She panicked at the sight of the dust. "I thought it was smoke. I
thought my car was on fire."

She screamed for help, terrified that the car was burning. She
thrust her hand out the broken window, frantically waving.

Warm fingers curled around hers and a gentle voice said, "It's
alright. You will be alright. Help is coming."

Deborah could not see the person who comforted her. "My arm
was slightly back," she said. "I couldn't turn around to look at them. I
felt an eerie calm."

Within minutes a state trooper had opened the passenger door
and was peering in at her. He told Deborah that everything was
going to be okay. As he reassured her, she felt the comforting hand
loosen its grip.

"I asked the trooper to tell whoever had been holding my hand to come around so I could see them and thank them," said Deborah.

But the trooper told her that no one had been holding her hand.

"Yes, there was!" she insisted. "They were talking to me!" The two argued about the existence of the Good Samaritan, and Deborah found herself getting frustrated. She knew she had not imagined the kind person and the warm hand that held hers.

The state trooper, however, was adamant. "Ma'am," he said. "There was no one around the car when I pulled up, and there is no one there now."

A cluster of people had gathered at the side of the road, but they were nervous about the possibility of an explosion and had stayed at least twenty feet away from the wreck.

The trooper told Deborah that he had seen her hand sticking out the window, but there had been no one nearby. Despite the fact that her hand had been out in the crisp air, it felt warm, as if someone *had* been holding it.

She *knew* someone had been with her, though she couldn't say whether the voice belonged to a man or woman. She knew only that it was soothing.

"I broke every bone in my foot in the accident, and the doctors told me that there was little chance I would walk again," said Deborah. If her foot were to recover, they added, it would take at least a year. But five months later, she proved them wrong and took her first step.

Despite her shattered foot, she was thankful for her life and relieved to learn that though the other driver was injured, he had also survived.

Deborah, a happily married mother of a grown son, works as a business support specialist for the army. A few years after the accident, the army chaplain stopped by her office, and she found herself sharing the story of the mysterious person who had held her hand.

"He sent an angel to watch over you that morning," the chaplain told her. "You should be very thankful he was watching over you that day."

Why didn't the angel *prevent* Deborah's accident?

No earthly being can be certain of the answer to that question, though many speculate that we must experience some suffering in order for our souls to evolve.

The teenager in the next case was burdened with tremendous emotional pain after her accident. She, too, questions why things turned out as they did. But she has shown remarkable strength as she forges ahead, trying to make the world better for others.

Buckled Up

LAST MINUTE DECISION SAVES LIFE.

Seventeen-year-old Mary Reinhart read the headline with a mixture of awe and confusion. The newspaper article was about her, the lone survivor in the car crash she would never forget. Not only would she never forget it, she would remember the details with excruciating clarity.

The newspaper got it mostly right, she thought, as she read the article about the night that changed her life. But there was one detail that puzzled her. She found herself reliving the crucial moment, again and again, trying to make sense of the fact that she survived. But try as she might, she could not find a logical explanation for what happened on Sunday, December 1, 2002.

It was midnight and Mary, her boyfriend, Matt, and two friends, Kyle and Jeremy, were racing through Deerfield, Wisconsin, with a cop on their tail. The pretty blond teenager sat in the backseat beside Jeremy and urged her boyfriend to slow down. The boys laughed at her concern. Matt was a skilled race car driver and confident behind the wheel.

It was a small town, and the police knew the kids and their car. They would be in trouble even if the cop didn't catch up with them. Maybe the boys were afraid the trouble would be worse if they were found with beer. Matt pressed his foot to the gas as the other boys rolled down the windows, letting in the freezing air, and tossed out the alcohol.

At Mary's home, her mother, Maria Reinhart, paced restlessly. *Something is wrong!* she thought. She'd been psychic since she was a little girl, and her intuition was especially keen when it came to her five children.

There was the time when Christopher was fourteen and had injured his arm. The doctor concluded it wasn't serious. Christopher said that it didn't hurt much, but Maria *knew* it was broken. "I told the doctor I wanted it X-rayed," Maria told me.

She was so insistent that the reluctant doctor finally agreed. Maria was right. Christopher's arm *was* broken.

And one night while working at her job as director of a group home, she had called a coworker and asked him to come in early to cover for her. "Something is going to happen to my kids!" she told him.

Again, Maria was right. Soon after she made the phone call, three of her children were on a bus that became a target for vandals with rocks. A rock smashed into a bus window, and the kids' faces were sprayed with glass. They weren't seriously injured, but they were shaken by the experience.

Now, on this icy December night, Mary's mother was really
scared. "I knew the kids were speeding," she confided. "I could *feel* it!"
She picked up the phone and called her daughter.

Yes, Mary told her when she answered the cell phone, they were
in the car, but they were all fine and they weren't speeding.

Her daughter's reassurance did not put Maria at ease. As she
hung up the phone, she could not settle the warning prickles that
rushed through her. A moment later, she called again, but this time
no one answered. She left a message: HEY, MARY, IT'S MOM! PUT ON
YOUR SEAT BELT!

Mary didn't like lying to her mother, but there was no sense
in having her worry. A typical teenager, she did not always heed
her mother's advice. She often found herself rolling her eyes at her
mother's psychic predictions.

But Mary was nervous as the car careened down the country
road. She wished Matt would slow down. She hadn't heard the
phone ring a second time, but as the boys laughed and tossed the
beer out the window, she noticed there was a message. She listened
to her mother's warning and snapped on her seat belt.

"Matt, please slow down!" she called out to him.

"I was behind the passenger seat and couldn't get Matt's
attention," she said. "I unbuckled the seat belt so I could lean
forward." She shouted into her boyfriend's ear, pleading with him to
stop speeding, but he was full of beer and bravado.

As the countryside flashed by the car windows, Mary's fear
escalated, and she grabbed Jeremy's hand with her left hand.
"I had my seat belt in my right hand, and it was still unbuckled,"
she told me.

Mary remained halfway on her feet, leaning toward the driver
when terror loomed before them. They had come to a T in the road,
but there was no time to turn.

In that split second, they knew they were about to crash. Kyle cursed.

The car rolled five times and came to rest right side up in a field. It was dead quiet, and Mary was alone in the car. "I tried to get up," she remembered. Something held her down. In the midst of her shock, Mary noticed her seat belt was buckled.

How did that happen? she wondered. She had been halfway out of her seat when they realized they were about to crash. "There had been no time to react," said Mary. There had been no time for her to sit down and buckle her seat belt. Yet the belt was snapped across her lap.

She unbuckled the belt, got out of the car, and saw things that would shade her nightmares for the rest of her life.

The three boys had been thrown from the car. Only Mary survived.

Today Mary is twenty-six and the mother of two young daughters. She has spoken to students at more than one hundred high school assemblies about the night the boys lost their lives.

"I'd always been afraid to talk in front of people, but with this it's different," she stressed. "If I can save the life of one person, then it's worth it."

Indeed, she has saved at least three lives with her warnings about speeding and alcohol and the importance of wearing seat belts. Three girls have written to her, all with the same message: "I am alive because of your speech."

"At one school, I had an entire football team crying and hugging me after my talk," she said.

Mary has been on television on the *Montel Williams Show* and featured in *Seventeen Magazine,* sharing the message about the importance of seat belts. But until now, neither she nor her mother has confided about the psychic premonition or the mysterious buckling of the seat belt.

As the headline said, LAST MINUTE DECISION SAVES LIFE. The decision to buckle that seat belt *did* save her life, but Mary does not know *whose* decision it was.

As we talked, she still sounded perplexed as she tried to figure out how in the world the belt was buckled. "I remembered every detail about that night, so why don't I remember buckling my seat belt?" she asked.

The timely warning about the seat belt from Mary's mother should have been miracle enough. But when Mary undid the seat belt, another miracle occurred. The belt was inexplicably re-buckled.

While the mystery baffles Mary, she is thankful she survived. "I believe in God," she said, adding that she expects to see her three friends in the afterlife. "I know that their souls are okay."

When angels intervene to save lives, they often disregard logic, leaving survivors with a sense of bewildered gratitude. The woman in the following story was on a mission to help others when angels implemented most unusual methods to spare her life.

Not There

Judith Rowland walked out of the Starbucks coffee shop. It was a hot October day in New Orleans, Louisiana, and she was admittedly a little tired. She was three weeks into her stint as a government liaison for the Salvation Army. She had traveled from her home in Cincinnati, Ohio, after seeing the TV news images of the destruction wrought by Hurricane Katrina, the August 2005 cyclone that ravaged the area and left 80 percent of New Orleans under water.

"I knew I had to do something," she confided.

She began as a volunteer, but the devastation was so extensive that the management requested that some of the volunteers come on board as full-time employees. Judith was asked to make a one-year commitment. "I was in charge of eleven parishes and sometimes lived out of my car, helping people," she said.

The occasional coffee break was a necessity to get her through the long and stressful days. Now, with coffee in hand, she headed back to the car she had parked on the opposite side of the street. The road was a long, straight stretch of four lanes, divided in the middle by a strip of grass. She got halfway across and paused on the grass. "I'm sure I must have looked for cars before I started across," she told me, still trying to make sense of what happened next. "I was in law enforcement for fifteen years, and I am a trained observer."

Indeed, she saw only empty lanes as she walked into the street. She was nearly across when an odd rush of wind moved by her. "I was wearing an A line skirt, and it flapped," she said. As the edge of her skirt lifted with the current, she heard the distinctive sound of the cloth hitting something. "The material hit something hard," she stressed.

Yet there was *nothing* there.

It was peculiar, but she had no time to question it, for the next two steps took her out of the street and right up next to the green pickup truck, parked in front of her car. A man in the truck spoke to her, his words drifting through the open window in a slow, southern drawl. "I slowed that car down for you," he said. He was an older black man with short salt-and-pepper hair. He sat in the driver's seat, staring straight ahead.

"His tone was very matter-of-fact," remembered Judith. He did not turn his head to look at her or attempt to make eye contact.

Judith broke into a sweat. Though the day was warm, this new heat seemed to come from within her. It was as if she were hit with a sudden fever. Shaking, she got into her car, shut the door, and placed her coffee into the cup holder.

What just happened? What was the old man talking about?

Then a puzzling thing occurred. Judith had a sudden, *new* memory of the preceding moments. In her mind's eye, she saw a big car racing toward her, passing so closely that her skirt was lifted in its wake. She *remembered* her skirt flapping against the metal of the car.

Yet Judith knew she had not seen a car when she stood in the street and felt that rush of wind. It was as if an invisible car had blown past her.

The two conflicting memories melted together.

She now knew that there *had* been a car. But during the critical moment, it was rendered invisible to her.

She had nearly been struck. Of that she was certain. And if she *had* been hit, she would have been seriously injured or killed.

She tried to make sense of the curious situation. She must have seen what was there, for she had had an actual memory of a speeding car! But her *eyes* had not registered the close call as she was experiencing it.

Why?

Perhaps, she suggested, "God shielded my eyes so I didn't make the wrong human move."

It's a good point. If she had seen the approaching car, she might have frozen. Considering the narrow miss, any delay on her part could have been fatal.

And if the car had been moving any faster, she would have been hit.

If the old man had indeed slowed that car, he surely was an angel.

As Judith sat there, trying to process the extraordinary occurrence, the old man drove away in his truck. For an instant, she thought about following him to try to get answers. But she sensed that something spiritual had occurred, and it was not to be questioned. The appropriate response was gratitude. She thanked God for saving her life.

"I believe very much in the spirit world," Judith said, adding that she is a nondenominational Christian. The near accident reminded her of a statement she had made just a few years before her time in New Orleans. She had been on a mission trip in Bulgaria, helping prostitutes get off the streets.

A local girl who worked as a translator had warned Judith about the danger of being near such busy streets with reckless drivers. The girl was worried that Judith could be hit by a car.

"God didn't bring me here to kill me," Judith had told her.

The near miss in New Orleans, said Judith, "confirmed what I had said."

Today Judith lives in Atlanta, Georgia, and works in disaster management for the Salvation Army. "God cared enough about me to save my life. How can I not have reverence? It is very comforting to know that I don't have to be in charge," said the happily married mother of a grown daughter. She has told few people about the car that nearly struck her but hopes that by sharing her story she will encourage others to have faith.

While the angel who helped Judith used an inventive method to save her life, the rescuer in the next account was just plain blunt.

Stowaway

It was an autumn night in the late 1960s, and Karen was returning to her home in Hopedale, Massachusetts, after entering her pet rabbits and guinea pigs in a competition in a show in Connecticut.

The teenager drove her white Dodge Dart with her pets in their crates in the backseat. "I was driving along a major highway in Connecticut," confided Karen Holmes, who is today a retired social studies teacher. "I was going to take an exit off the highway when suddenly a loud voice yelled, "Pull over! Stop!"

Stunned, she pulled over. The disembodied voice seemed to come from within the car, but, of course, she was alone with her pets. The animals took up all the room in the backseat. She had stacked them there herself and knew that there was no room for a stowaway to hide.

"The voice was masculine and very upset," she told me. She felt she had had no choice but to obey the command. "I was completely unnerved," she said.

As she sat in her parked car, trying to calm herself down, another vehicle passed by, headed toward the exit. "A car was coming in the opposite direction," said Karen. "It was going the wrong way on the exit ramp. The car that passed me hit it head on. People in other cars stopped to help, but I was so traumatized I could do nothing but sit there."

Soon ambulances and police were on the scene, and Karen continued on her journey home. "I don't know what happened to the people in the wreck," she said. She felt sad for them but was grateful to the mysterious voice who warned her. "I believe the voice saved me from an accident," she said.

Vehicles don't need engines to be dangerous. Many folks report close calls on bicycles, and some insist that angels helped them escape injury.

In the next story, an angel was nearby when a young girl's bike ride took a bad turn.

A Light Place

Eleven-year-old Heather Clark grinned as she admired her shiny, black bike. It was a boy's bike, but that didn't matter. "It was my first new bike," she said, as she remembered the hot summer afternoon in Battleground, Washington.

Her parents had surprised her and her older brothers with new bikes, and the kids could not wait to ride them.

But they were not content to simply ride the bikes up and down the quiet street. Soon they were daring each other to jump the ditches. One by one, they raced toward a ditch and yanked the handlebars back at the last moment so they could sail through the air and land with a thud on the other side.

A group of neighbor kids gathered to watch as Heather took her turn. She pedaled toward the ditch but hesitated at the last instant. "I realized I was going too slowly," she said. "I knew I wasn't going to make it, so I put on the brakes. The back brake failed, and the front brake worked *too* well!"

She slammed to a stop, her stomach hitting the handlebars as she tipped forward. A moment later, she was on the ground. Dazed, she stood up. "I'd hit the handlebars so hard that they were bent at an angle!" she said. She took a couple of steps, and then everything went black.

The others laughed as they watched Heather fall. They thought that she was joking around, pretending to be hurt. They had no idea that the force of the impact had ruptured her gallbladder.

Suddenly Heather found herself meeting the gaze of a little boy. The blond boy with the solemn, gray eyes appeared to be four or five. "We didn't have any young kids in the neighborhood," Heather told me. "I thought, *He's not from here. He's not from our neighborhood!* I wondered where he had come from. He stood at my feet; his hands were cupped in front of him as if he were holding a baby bird."

Heather Pennick will never forget the celestial being who appeared to her during a dark moment. (Leslie Rule)

The child wore a long, white smock, and Heather noted that he had bangs, cut straight across his forehead. He stood in an oval of white light. "The rest of the world was gray," said Heather. The ditch, the mangled bike, her brothers, and the neighbor kids had all vanished.

"The boy was in a light place. We looked directly at each other, and I was filled with peace," she confided. "It was as if he was saying, 'It's going to be okay.'"

Meanwhile, Heather's father was running toward her. He had been working in the yard and had watched her ill-fated attempt to jump the ditch.

Bill Clark noted that his daughter's limp body was turning blue. *Heather was not breathing!* He began to perform mouth-to-mouth resuscitation.

The angelic, golden-haired child abruptly vanished, and Heather found herself staring up at the face of her frantic father. The pain hit. "I started crying for my mom," said Heather.

She was rushed to St Joseph's Hospital in Vancouver, Washington, where doctors discovered that in addition to her ruptured gallbladder, she had also bruised her liver.

"I was in the hospital for days, and when I got home, I went to my room and saw my bike set up there." She took one look at the bent handlebars and shuddered.

"I've never ridden a bike again," said Heather Pennick, who is now thirty-five and the mother of two daughters. But something good came out of the experience. "I got to see an angel. I know someone is looking out for me."

Heather's encounter with the angelic boy could have been a near-death experience (NDE). The oval of white light that she described could have been the entrance to the proverbial tunnel that leads to the world beyond and the boy her escort, ready to take her on the ultimate journey.

It is said that angels escort us when we leave our bodies and prepare to venture to a wondrous place that we, for now, can only imagine. The next chapter will explore cases that give us a glimpse of the glorious place that awaits us.

Chapter Nine
GLIMPSE
OF HEAVEN

I SAW THE ANGEL IN THE MARBLE,
AND I CARVED UNTIL I SET HIM FREE.

—*Michelangelo* (1475–1564), ITALIAN RENAISSANCE ARTIST

Some people fear death. But those who have "died" and come
back to life tell us that there is nothing to be afraid of. They describe
a place where angels tread that is filled with light and love and the
spirits of our deceased friends and relatives.

Most folks who have glimpsed the afterlife are changed afterward.
They might be more patient and accepting of others. Material things
are no longer as important to them as they once were.

Sometimes they are inspired.

While researching this book, I came across three cases of people
who had momentarily died and were so inspired by what they had

experienced that they were moved to share their visions through creativity.

One is an artist, one is a writer, and one is a musician.

Just as Michelangelo saw an angel in a cold block of marble and was driven to set him free, the creators who experienced near-death were compelled to set *their* angels free.

Andy Lakey is a Ventura, California, artist known for his abstract angel paintings. Earlier in his life he was heavily involved with dangerous drugs. On New Year's Eve in 1985, he was freebasing cocaine when he overdosed and found himself on his shower floor. He saw "seven twirling angels," and he promised God that if he survived he would give up drugs.

The angels, he has said, told him to paint angels and that they would guide him, teaching him to paint.

Today the man who had never previously picked up a paintbrush has his work showcased in galleries around the planet, with his very first painting displayed in the Vatican. Some claim that they receive spiritual guidance simply by touching his work.

Pastor Don Piper authored the best-selling book *90 Minutes in Heaven* fifteen years after he "died." It was the middle of the day in January 1989, and the Pasadena, Texas, pastor, thirty-nine, was headed home after attending a conference when he was hit head on by an eighteen-wheeler as he traveled over a bridge.

His Ford Escort was crushed, and he was pronounced dead. Emergency respondents covered him with a tarp.

A fellow pastor, Dick Onerecker of Kline, Texas, came upon the accident and was moved to pray over the body of his dead friend. He held Don's limp hand and sang hymns until the deceased man woke up.

Nearly every bone in his body was broken, but he survived. He endured thirty-four surgeries to repair the damage, which included the rebuilding of severed limbs.

For years he guarded his near-death experience as a "sacred secret," but fellow pastors eventually persuaded him to write about it.

In *90 Minutes in Heaven,* Pastor Piper wrote about meeting angels along with the welcoming spirits of friends and relatives. He also described a large gate that appeared to be sculpted from mother-of-pearl. He was awestruck by the sound of an angelic choir and longed to move beyond the gate to meet God.

Award-winning recording artist Christian Andreason nearly died in June 1995 while undergoing dental surgery. His prescription medicine interacted with the anesthetic, causing his blood pressure to plummet.

The Houston, Texas, singer has since spoken openly about his NDE and the influence it has had on his music. He was "gone" for just two earthly minutes, but from his perspective, the journey was timeless. He saw Heaven and met spiritual beings and sensed an overpowering love that changed the way he viewed music. He vowed to write and record uplifting songs, and today he favors music with "strong, flowing, melodic lines and positive lyrics" that are healing to the soul.

We corresponded about his near-death angelic encounters, and he wrote, "Angels are the keepers of music." He went on to say that celestial beings use music to heal us and keep us from harm.

According to Christian, many different kinds of angels exist, including very large, warrior angels. They are, he said, between twelve and twenty feet tall.

⌒⌒

In September 1980, a shirttail relative of mine died at age fifty-seven when his homemade sauna exploded on his property in Mason County, Washington. Ira died instantly. His nephew told me that his uncle had not feared death but had actually looked forward to the ultimate journey, for he believed there were adventures to be had in the afterlife.

His family was reassured when they talked to the young woman who survived the accident. She had been sitting beside Ira in the sauna and had seen his spirit walk away. In fact, she *followed* him. She was right behind him as he headed down a long tunnel.

Ira suddenly stopped and turned around, "You go back," he said. "Your daughter needs you!"

He was right. The little girl needed her mother.

Ira's twin sister, Mary, told me that the woman had heeded his advice and that the next thing she knew, she was back in her body.

The image of the long tunnel with the light at the end is familiar to most Americans. Though few of us have yet to travel through the tunnel, millions of us have read Dr. Raymond Moody's book *Life After Life*. First published in 1975, the book features case studies of people who were momentarily "clinically dead" and glimpsed the afterlife. Most reported that they had traveled down a long tunnel or hallway, headed toward a bright light.

My father died of skin cancer at the young age of forty-three, the same year Dr. Moody's book was published, and I found great comfort as I read the eyewitness accounts of a wonderful world beyond.

I've since known a few people who had their own NDEs, including Anita Porterfield of Borne, Texas. She jokes that she was born with "ink in her veins." She has been involved in some aspect of publishing since the age of thirteen. She is currently the book editor and a contributing writer for *The Borne Star*.

Anita is not afraid to die. She has done so more than once. When I asked her to describe the events, here is what she wrote:

A statue of an angel holds a flaming torch at The Grotto in Portland, Oregon. (Leslie Rule)

Flat Line

BY ANITA PORTERFIELD

Caught in the beauty of the moment, I hovered, suspended in a primordial mist, unencumbered by space or time. Movement was effortless, and I joined a group of people below me. I knew them. They were my family, and I was surrounded by love. I was home.

I opened my eyes. "Hey!" *I shouted.* "Quit! Don't wake me up! I was having a wonderful dream." *I couldn't understand why my husband, John, was shaking me.*

My dream was unlike any other that I had ever had. It stayed with me for days. The people in my dream were familiar, but I could not remember where or when we had been together.

A month later, on a cold February Saturday morning, I had a similar dream. This time I saw a large, round table with several men sitting around it. My father and some of his buddies were playing poker, laughing and talking. My father ordered me to leave, to "Go back." *I told him that I didn't want to leave.*

Again, my husband shook me until I awakened and, again, I was very upset that he had interrupted my dream.

On a Sunday morning in March, I poured myself a second cup of coffee. Without warning, I was suddenly transported back to the place in my first dream. This time I awoke in a hospital, wires sprouting from my chest, the sound of monitors filling the room. John was sitting in a chair by the bed, holding my hand.

"How did I get here?" *I asked him.*

"You fell backwards onto the tile floor in the kitchen," *he told me.* "You have a concussion. Don't you remember?" *he asked.* "I put you in the car and drove you here. You talked about your dream."

I didn't remember anything.

A handsome woman in her mid-fifties walked into the room and identified herself as a neurologist. My family doctor had asked her to see me.

She asked me some questions about my fall. Did I feel faint before I passed out? Had I been having headaches? Did I see lights before I fell?

My answers to her questions were, "No." I had no warning. I felt nothing.

Despite my insistence on leaving the hospital, I was probed, scanned, and tested for five days. The good news was that I was healthy. The bad news was that they could not determine what had caused me to lose consciousness.

I went home with a portable cardiac monitor around my neck and electrodes attached to my chest. I was to wear the device until I "fainted" again or for up to three weeks. I was instructed to push the RECORD *button if I felt lightheaded. The monitor would record my cardiac activity for several minutes, after which I was to call a central monitoring facility and send my recorded EKG via the telephone.*

Three weeks later, on a beautiful Sunday morning, John and I were outside discussing renovations on our house. It was the final day that I had to put up with the monitor. Suddenly I realized I was laying flat on the ground. John hovered over me.

"You fainted again," he told me as he picked me up and carried me into the house.

"I had that dream again," I said. "It was wonderful, and I didn't want to wake up." He sat me down in a kitchen chair, removed the monitor, and transmitted the recording.

"Did I push the button?" I asked.

"No," he said. "You didn't have time. I pushed it."

The phone rang and John answered. It was the monitoring facility. I was to go to the hospital immediately.

In the emergency room, a doctor whom I had never seen before walked into the cubicle holding a strip of paper. "Do you know what this is?" he asked, handing the strip to me.

"It's a flatline EKG," I responded. I had worked as an EMT years earlier and was familiar with electrocardiograms.

"It's your flat line," he said. "You were clinically dead. You have a cardiac arrhythmia that causes your heart to stop. You are lucky to have a husband who knows CPR. You need a pacemaker."

I've now had my pacemaker for seven years. I no longer fear death and am certain that life continues on in the spirit world.

Friends and family have told me that I have an unfulfilled purpose in life, that I survived for a reason, and it was not my time to die. I don't know about that, but I do cherish life more than I did before the heart-stopping episodes. I wake up every day with gratitude and with a renewed determination to make each day count.

After reading Anita's account, some may wonder if they *really* have poker in Heaven. Her father had enjoyed it immensely in life. Playing eternal poker probably *was* his idea of Heaven!

When it comes to glimpses of the spirit world, however, the things seen may simply take on the form of what we can understand. Perhaps in the afterlife we are pure energy and exist without bodies. While we straddle life and death, we are able to feel the love and tranquility from beyond but don't yet have the vision to understand the ways of the new realm.

Skeptics theorize that the classic NDE is nothing more than a hallucination caused by lack of oxygen. But that theory is ragged around the edges.

How do the skeptics explain the fact that so many people are able to accurately describe the scene of their near-deaths?

Many near-death patients remember hovering over their bodies, watching from above. How can a woman, unconscious beside her wrecked car, later give detailed descriptions of the people who rushed to rescue her?

How can a man who clinically died in his hospital bed remember seeing objects on top of the room's armoire that no one should be able to see without a stepladder?

The skeptics stubbornly hold onto their doubts and will likely not be convinced until the day that they, too, step into the tunnel and head toward the bright light.

I wonder if they will tell themselves that they are just dreaming when they meet the angels and spirits of their loved ones, who will surely be there to greet them.

According to most of those who have experienced near-death, celestial escorts from the world beyond are ready to welcome us. Often, the spirits urge the dying person's soul to go back to their body.

Angels and spirits have also been sensed by those keeping deathbed vigils. It seems that as we live our last hours, heavenly beings surround us.

A doctor who worked in oncology and saw many patients take their last breaths told me it was common for them to suddenly call out a name, as if greeting an old friend. Their families were not always present for the deaths, so the doctor would later describe the final moments to them.

"I began to see a pattern," she said. "When I told the families the names I heard, they would tell me that it was the name of a relative who had died. And it was very common for them to tell me that the name belonged to a pet. The family members would say something like, 'Cooper? That was the dog he had forty years ago when he was ten years old!'"

It is reassuring to think our pets will be there to greet us, welcoming us to Heaven. I've had countless pets and will likely have a menagerie waiting for me.

Several days before this writing, I had to say good-bye to Siren, one of my elderly cats. She was a sweet, petite calico of pastel shades.

I wanted to give her every chance, but the veterinarians told me that she was "a very sick kitty" and was in great discomfort. There was nothing more they could do, they said. So I sat in the vet's office and held her for about twenty minutes as we waited for the doctor to come in to help her along.

My mother was with me and held the oxygen cup close to the cat's face, as the vet had asked us to do. Siren's breathing was labored, and she was very still in my arms. But about two minutes before the

Siren lived a long life, and seemed to see someone visible only to her moments before she crossed over to the other side. (Leslie Rule)

doctor entered the room, Siren suddenly became alert and lifted her head to gaze intently at something only she could see. And then she turned and looked over my shoulder, her yellow eyes opening wide, as if she saw someone standing behind me.

"What is she looking at?" I asked my mother. "She sees someone."

Siren had been my cat for the past six months and had lived with my mother for the five years before that. And before *that* she had spent ten years in another home. She had shown up there, as an adult stray, sixteen years ago.

We didn't know her exact age or the identity of her first owner. For all we knew, they were long dead. Perhaps it was the spirit of Siren's former owner, coming for her. Or perhaps it was her feline mother.

Or maybe it was an angel.

Pets can't tell us when they see angels, but that doesn't mean that they don't encounter them. I like to think that an angel came for Siren.

When the body fails and death is inevitable, angels gather around. As I listen to accounts of celestial beings sensed by those who have held deathbed vigils, I visualize the door to the other side cracking open. The angels peek in and then, one by one, form a group of heavenly escorts. They join the vigil, but they are not there to say good-bye. They are there to say hello.

Sometimes the relatives of the dying witness the angels, but in most cases, only the terminal patient sees them, as in the next story.

Prayer Circle

In the last days of her mother's life, Angelica Rodriguez slept on the floor beside her bed in their Bayamon, Puerto Rico, home. It was very early one morning in June 2009 when she was roused from a deep sleep by the sound of her mother's voice.

She was surprised to see her sitting up in bed. Ana, fifty-three, had been fighting cancer for the last decade. Angie had been only fourteen when her mother got sick, but she did not complain when she became her caretaker.

Ana Rodriguez was so frail she could barely move without assistance, so Angie could not understand how she had managed to sit up on her own.

"She asked me, 'Who are those people?'" Angie told me.

Ana told her daughter that there was a group of people in the room.

"I was really scared at first because I didn't know what she was talking about," Angie confided. "Then for some reason, I calmed."

Ana, too, was calm. "She was so peaceful," remembered Angie. "She wasn't scared, but she was curious."

She was also a little frustrated with her daughter when she denied seeing anyone. The sick woman pointed a bony finger and, speaking in her native language, asked "Don't you see them?"

"I looked in the direction she was pointing," said Angie. "But I didn't see anything."

The people, Ana told her daughter, shined from within and were dressed in white. "She said that they were by her side, praying."

Her mother told her that though she could hear their voices, she did not understand them. It was as if the angelic beings were praying in a foreign tongue. Some of them were on their knees praying. One feminine being was right beside her, her head bowed, while others were standing.

"I helped her to lie down again and asked her to go to sleep," Angie said. "It was 2:30 A.M."

When daylight brightened the room, Ana awoke again. Angie decided not to mention the bizarre episode. She was sure it must have been an odd, waking dream that her mother would not remember. But Ana was still excited and had perfect recollection of her visitors.

Angelica Rodriguez and her mother in one of the rare photos she has of them together. (Photo courtesy of Angelica Rodriguez)

"I was shocked," said Angie. "She hadn't been dreaming, and she was still very frustrated with my lack of vision!"

When Angie told her cousin what had happened, she suggested that the "people" were actually angels and that they were preparing to take Ana to Heaven.

Though it saddened Angie to think her mother's time on earth was coming to an end, she was comforted to know that the angels would be with her.

"My mom loved angels and always believed that angels took care of her," she said. "She told me that they are beautiful and strong. She believed in the afterlife and ghosts and angels."

The beings who appeared to Ana were definitely not the spirits of deceased relatives, Angie decided, for her mother had not recognized them.

"I'm sorry that I couldn't see them, but maybe when my time comes, I will," she ventured. "I'm not scared of death anymore because I know that my mom will receive me on the other side."

About a week after the angels appeared, Ana passed away. Angie's grief was softened by the knowledge that her mother was with the angels.

Glimpse of Heaven in the News

"HEAVEN LOOKED NICE"

WHEN A THREE-YEAR-OLD German boy was found beneath the water in his grandparents' pond in April 2010, his chances of survival were slim. A number of newspapers, including Germany's *Bild,* reported that Paul Eicke was submerged for more than three minutes in the pond in Lychen, Brandenburg, Germany, before he was discovered by his grandfather.

The child's father massaged his heart and performed mouth-to-mouth resuscitation as a helicopter flew to the scene. Paul was airlifted to the Helios Hospital in Buch, on the outskirts of Berlin, where doctors worked on him for three hours and eighteen minutes and were about to abandon hope when little Paul's heart began beating.

Dr. Lothar Schweigerer, the hospital director, told reporters that the fact that the boy survived and suffered no brain damage was "a fantastic miracle," explaining that doctors had continued the resuscitation effort as long as they had because the cold water had lowered Paul's core temperature enough to slow down his metabolism, which allowed him to live longer without oxygen.

Dr. Schweigerer said, "I've been doing this job for thirty years and have never seen anything like it."

The boy told his parents that "there was a lot of light, and I was floating," describing how he had seen a gate with his great-grandmother Emmie on the other side. She had asked him what he was doing there and then insisted that he hurry home to "Mummy and Daddy," assuring him that she would be waiting there for him.

"Grandma said I had to come home," Paul explained, adding, "Heaven looked nice, but I am glad I am back with Mummy and Daddy now."

PROOF OF LIFE BEYOND

IN THEIR DECEMBER 2001 issue, *New Scientist* magazine reported that a Dutch cardiologist conducted an in-depth study of NDEs and concluded that there is no medical explanation for the phenomenon.

Dr. Pim Van Lommel of Arnhem, Holland, interviewed 344 patients who had momentarily died during cardiac arrest, and he found that 18 percent reported an NDE. The doctor published the results of his study in the respected medical journal *The Lancet*.

The patients reported such things as hovering over their bodies, seeing or entering a tunnel with a light at the end, and encountering angels and spirits of relatives.

Dr. Van Lommel found no connection between NDEs and the patients' prescribed medications. He dismissed skeptics' claims that the NDE is a result of the dying brain's lack of oxygen and said, "If there were a physiological cause, all the patients should have had an NDE."

The doctor followed up, interviewing the subjects throughout the next decade, and noted that most of the survivors had developed a new level of sensitivity and compassion and that they remembered their experiences with surprising clarity.

Dr. Van Lommel later wrote a book about his case studies, *Consciousness Beyond Life: The Science of the Near-Death Experience*, published in English in 2011.

Chapter Ten

LIGHT
IN THE DARK

FOR EACH MOMENT OF
HORROR IN THE WORLD
WE FIND THESE ACTS OF GOODNESS,
BY THE HANDS OF ANGELS.

—*Sophy Burnham,* AUTHOR OF *A Book of Angels*

Of all the dangers we humans face, perhaps the scariest are those wrought by our fellow man.

I believe that most people are basically good. Oh, we have our faults. But most of us will help others when there is a need. And it is the rare person who actually wants to harm another.

Those rare people seem to walk in darkness, casting cold shadows wherever they go. Some are simply insane, while others possess minds that science has yet to understand. They prey on others, sometimes taking lives. It is horrendous, but we can take comfort in knowing that their victims' souls live on.

And then there are the victims who manage to escape. Sometimes it is through their own cunning and strength that they manage to survive.

And sometimes it is with the help of an angel.

Lynette Grace of Columbus, Ohio, sent me the following account of a terrifying night when she found herself caught between good and evil.

Lynette wrote,

In August 1991 I was living in Atlanta, Georgia, when my father called me with sad news. My mother had died of a heart attack. Soon, I was on a plane, headed toward my parents' Toledo, Ohio, home.

After the funeral, I called my good friend, Eddie Laura Bell. She lived in Columbus, Ohio, where I had once lived. Both devout Christians, we had met in church.

Sister Bell opened her home to me, inviting me to stay for a couple of days and to attend church with her and her family. We had dinner together and enjoyed a nice conversation before I retired to her guest room.

Around six a.m. something woke me. I heard a scuffling sound. I thought I was dreaming, and then I heard Sister Bell's agitated voice. "Johnny, no!"

I got up to see what was going on. I put on my glasses and walked toward the door. I opened it slowly and peeked through the crack. I saw Johnny, Sister Bell's sixteen-year-old son, standing in the doorway across the hall. He was in his underwear.

I assumed that Johnny and his mother must have had an argument. Since I was just a visitor, I didn't want to pry into their personal business, but I was worried about Sister Bell so I asked, "Johnny, is Sister Bell having a bad dream?"

"Yeah," he said. "She's having a bad dream."

I paused and nodded, not knowing what to say or do next. "Do you want me to go downstairs to see if there is anything I can do for her?"

"Yeah," he said.

I walked past him and through the house. Her voice had seemed to be coming from the basement, so I headed down the stairs. I expected to hear her crying, but it was very quiet. I walked past the laundry room and the recreation room. I turned the corner, and there was Sister Bell. She was face down, on the floor, covered in blood.

I sensed Johnny standing next to me. "Johnny, what happened?" I gasped.

"I don't know." His demeanor was oddly calm.

My mind raced. Had someone broken in and attacked her? I glanced at the phone. Johnny seemed to read my mind. "Oh," he said. "I've already called 9-1-1."

But the receiver had been ripped from the phone. Johnny's story didn't add up. I was terrified, but I knew Sister Bell needed help. I ran up the stairs, toward the kitchen phone. Johnny got there before I could. He blocked the doorway.

He struck me with something, knocking my glasses off. I tried to catch them, but they slipped through my fingers.

The situation was confusing, but I was certain of one thing: Johnny had hurt his mother. My vision is so bad that without my glasses, I could not see him. I was petrified. I didn't know what to do.

Then a quiet voice spoke to me. "Make him think you can see him."

The disembodied voice could not be characterized as either male or female. It was simply a reassuring voice, speaking close to my ear.

I faced Johnny and looked in his direction.

"Calm him down," urged the voice.

In a soothing tone I said, "Johnny, everything is going to be alright." I repeated my words, talking to him as if he were a small child who had lost his toy. He continued to strike me, but I continued to try to comfort him. Suddenly, he stopped, dropped his head, and walked down the hallway.

All I could do was stand there, frozen to the spot, until the voice shouted a command. "Go!"

I turned and ran out the back door and into the darkness of the early morning. I ran to the neighbors' house for help, and soon the police arrived. My friend was beyond help, but I know that her spirit is in Heaven.

Johnny was sentenced to a maximum of forty years in prison.

Every day I thank God for my life. I know he sent an angel to help me on that terrifying night.

In Lynette's case, her rescuer needed only a voice to help her. Sometimes our helpers from beyond don't speak but simply appear. And that is all that is necessary to assist us, as in the following case.

Sweet Warning

Sharon Henderson wanted candy. It was a summer evening in 1977, and she and her sister both worked as counselors at a horse camp in the foothills of Battlecreek, Washington. The camp owners served only health food, so when Sharon craved sweets she drove into town to stock up on junk food.

She had had the afternoon off and had visited friends in the area before making her trip to the store. "I always stopped at the same convenience store and bought candy," remembered Sharon, who today lives in Albuquerque, New Mexico, with her teenage daughter.

As she pulled into the parking lot, an overwhelming sense of dread washed over her. She tried to shrug it off. "I was only eighteen, but it took a lot to unnerve me," she stressed. "I'd traveled around the country by myself and knew I could take care of myself."

Yet she could not shake her apprehension. She glanced about, looking for something amiss in the parking lot. Everything seemed to be in order. "There was not a person in sight," she told me. "I thought, *This is ridiculous. I want candy!*"

She chose a parking spot by the front door. "I put the car in park, but the engine was still running," she recalled. She looked up and was startled to see a figure standing outside the door, as if guarding the entryway. The apparition was translucent and manifested from the shoulders up.

"I could not tell if it was a man or a woman, but I clearly saw a head and shoulders," said Sharon.

The figure shook its head, as if in warning. The message was clear: Sharon was not to enter the store. "I put the car in reverse and turned the car around," she said.

(Leslie Rule)

Still, she questioned her own eyes. "I glanced back one more time just to be sure I was not being unduly silly, but the figure was still there. That's when I got really scared. It was as if it were saying, 'No! Go away!'"

But it was not the figure itself that frightened her. Despite the fact it was certainly unusual to see part of a transparent person, there was nothing menacing about the mysterious being. Sharon instinctively sensed it was protecting her from an unknown danger.

She drove quickly through the parking lot and headed back to camp.

The next day she heard shocking news. The convenience store had been robbed. A gunman was there at the same time that Sharon had stopped for candy. He had shot and killed the clerk.

Sharon was horrified. "My first thought was for the victim," she said. "I felt guilty because I was there at the time of the robbery. I thought that maybe I could have done something to help."

But an unsuspecting teenage girl was no match for an armed killer. She had no way to know there was a robbery in progress, and if she had blundered in, she too could have been a victim.

"I've told very few people about this," said Sharon, who is still in awe of the night her sweet tooth led her to danger and spiritual intervention saved her life.

(Leslie Rule)

Angels Fighting Evil in the News

AN ENTIRE SCHOOL of children was rescued by angels who appeared when a madman took them hostage on May 16, 1986.

The miracle occurred at the Cokeville Elementary School in Cokeville, Wyoming, and put the small town on the map.

David Young, who had been relieved of his job as the town's lone police officer six years earlier, arrived at the school with guns and a bomb and terrorized the children and teachers. His wife, Doris, gathered everyone into one classroom, and many of the frightened children began to pray as the couple threatened them.

The children later reported that bright angels in white clothing appeared and ushered them to an area near the windows, moments before Doris accidentally triggered the bomb. The blast killed her. Shortly afterward, David Young shot himself.

All the teachers and children escaped with their lives.

Investigators found that the wires on some of the most deadly detonators had been inexplicably severed, rendering them powerless. (Sources include the *Deseret News* and the book *When Angels Intervene to Save the Children,* coauthored by Hartt and Judene Wixom, parents of one of the young hostages.)

ANGELS FOR THE ENEMY WITHIN

SOMETIMES THE DARKNESS comes from within, and we become our own enemies. Depressed people might believe that death is the only way out.*

But naysayers warn that suicide does not end our problems. We may have to work through our issues in the afterlife. Or we may be sent back here to relive the same troubling sequence of events.

Sometimes those determined to discard their bodies are stopped in miraculous ways. Who would think that a person could survive a 400-foot plunge? When a twenty-two-year-old man leapt from the thirty-ninth floor of a building in New York in the summer of 2010, he crushed the Dodge Charger he landed on, but he lived. The young man flew feet first through the windshield as shocked onlookers watched.

The car's owner, construction worker Gary McCormack, showed up soon after and retrieved his crystal rosary beads from within his destroyed automobile. He waved the beads at reporters and shouted, "Here's what saved him!"

Though the jumper was hospitalized in critical condition, he was up and walking within three months.

*National Suicide Hotline: (800) 273-TALK (8255).

Chapter Eleven
ANIMAL
MIRACLES

IT AMAZES ME THAT ANIMALS
SEE ANGELS SO EASILY.

—*Lorna Byrne*, AUTHOR OF *Angels in My Hair*

We shouldn't be surprised when an animal saves a human life. Animals are far more sensitive and intelligent than most people believe.

I've always been in tune with animals—so much so that I have been a vegetarian since age seventeen, and though I am well aware that animals are perceptive creatures with hearts and souls, I was astonished by some of the cases I found of furry heroism.

While researching this book, I scoured newspaper archives for stories of miraculous pet heroics, and I stumbled upon a case of a dog rescuing an abandoned infant.

As always, I looked for as many sources as possible to verify the facts. As I did so, I noticed discrepancies between some of the news articles and at first thought that the reporters had made blatant mistakes. But as I looked closer, I realized I had found not one but three separate cases of dogs saving discarded babies.

But it didn't stop there. I soon had so many accounts of dogs saving abandoned babies that I could fill an entire book. I've chosen to mention three cases.

In the summer of 2003, a sheepdog in Raducaneni, Romania, woke his owner from a sound sleep with his persistent barks and scratches at the front door.

Elena Florea opened the door to see her big dog, Vasile, looking at her expectantly. When she saw what he had brought her, she shrieked. The big dog hovered over a newborn baby who was bundled in swaddling clothes.

"I called the mayor's office immediately," Elena Florea told a reporter, explaining that she feared her dog had gone into someone's house and snatched the infant.

But Vasile was no kidnapper. He was a hero.

When police investigated, they discovered the spot where the baby had been abandoned. It was a remote field, two miles from the canine's home. The noble dog had apparently found the crying infant and gingerly carried him through the dark of night to the safety of his owner's stoop.

Another poor child was left for dead in a plastic bag in a Kenya forest in May 2005. If not for a very maternal stray dog who was out foraging for food for her puppies, the tiny girl would not have lived.

The medium-sized, mixed-breed dog removed the child from the bag and carried the seven-pound, four-ounce infant across a busy street and through a barbed-wire fence to her nest behind a rundown shack in a poor neighborhood.

A witness told reporters he had heard crying and had seen the dog carrying the child across the street. Later, two children heard the wails of the newborn and told their parents. When the concerned adults investigated, they found the infant beside the dog and her one surviving puppy.

Authorities assured reporters that the baby girl was doing well at Kenyatta National Hospital, where health-care workers called her Angel. Animal welfare officials gave the mother dog her first bath and a deworming. They named her Mkombozi, which translates to Savior.

About three years later, in August 2008, an eight-pound, thirteen-ounce baby boy was discarded in a garbage-strewn field in La Plata, Argentina. The fourteen-year-old mother was poverty stricken and terrified. She made the dark decision to abandon her baby.

Temperatures dipped to thirty-seven degrees that night, and the naked newborn would have been doomed if not for the miracle of motherly instinct.

While the young girl who deserted her baby had no such instinct, a four-footed mother named China had more than enough maternal instinct to go around. She must have heard the baby whimpering, for she carried him 150 feet and deposited him in the middle of her litter of six puppies.

The infant survived the night, thanks to the heat generated by the canine family. China's surprised owner looked in on his dogs in the morning and found the baby boy, snuggling with the puppies.

Who knows if there is something more than a protective instinct that guides dogs to save helpless babies? Maybe angels are at work, nudging the canines toward the infants who need them. That certainly seemed to be the case in the following story, when the situation was flipped and a helpless puppy needed a human's assistance.

The Puppy's Angel

It was an icy morning in Bessemer, Alabama, and a lost puppy desperately needed help. The little chow mix was barely seven weeks old and had somehow become separated from his mother and littermates.

Trying to find his way, he had apparently tromped through a ditch filled with iced-over water. The wet dog then tried to cross the railroad tracks. But it was freezing cold. The thermostat had dropped to fourteen degrees.

No one knows exactly how the puppy got into his predicament on January 9, 2010. Perhaps he had stopped to rest a moment on the train track's metal rail. Or maybe it was cold enough that all it took was brief contact of wet fur on metal to create an icy bond. However it happened, the puppy became frozen to the tracks. He was in danger of freezing to death—if the train didn't reach him first. The puppy, of course, did not know what a train was. And he could not know that the next one was due to zoom through in an hour. His chances did not look good. He needed a miracle.

Approximately seven miles away, Gary McLean, a track inspector for CSX Railroad, was starting his workday. It was his job to drive a rail truck along the tracks, knocking debris from the rails. "Kids like to put rocks on the tracks," he told me, explaining that a flap on the front of the truck brushes small objects off the rails.

Track inspectors coordinate their routes with the railroad dispatcher, and this day Gary was given a route that would take him north along the tracks. But as he prepared to start, he hesitated.

Something did not *feel* right. "I thought I should be going north to south," he confided. The idea was so overpowering that Gary called the dispatcher, who agreed to send him in the opposite direction.

After nearly three years on the job, Gary knew the terrain. It was so familiar that he anticipated each dip and bump on the route. As he traveled along a stretch of smooth track that morning, something unusual happened. "I was riding along at about fifteen to twenty miles an hour when the truck jerked and shuddered," said Gary. "It felt like I had run over something. I thought, 'What the heck was that?'"

But when he looked back, he saw nothing. "My truck has never done that before," he said. As he prepared to proceed, something caught his eye. It was just a few feet ahead, a small brown thing that blended in because it was the same color as the tracks. "It looked like a dead animal. I got out of the truck and I saw that it was a puppy." A dog lover with three of his own at home, Gary was saddened by the sight of what he assumed was a deceased dog.

"I tried to pick him up, and that's when I realized the little guy was frozen, stuck to the rails." Big brown eyes looked up at Gary. The puppy was alive.

Gary tried to melt the ice by spraying water on the rail and the shivering dog's paws and chest. But the water became ice the instant it hit the rail.

He got out his pocketknife and cautiously slid the blade between the puppy's fur and the metal. In a moment, he was free and in the loving arms of a man who rushed him to the warmth of the truck, dried him off, and wrapped him in his extra coat.

Gary knew that something miraculous had taken place. An inexplicable feeling had compelled him

Gary McLean snapped this picture within minutes of finding the puppy.

to call the dispatcher and change his route. If he had stuck with the original plan to travel north, no one would have found the puppy before the train came through.

Gary's truck was just a few feet away from running over the little creature when the vehicle had gone over a bump that did not exist. If the truck had not lurched to a stop, he would not have noticed the puppy until it was too late.

With the dog on the seat beside him, Gary backed up the truck, trying to find a cause for the mysterious occurrence. "There was nothing. I could not find anything that would cause the truck to shudder like that."

Could it have been angelic intervention?

Yes, according to Gary. "I believe in angels," he told me.

"Who helped the puppy that day?" I asked him. "Was it your angel, or the puppy's angel?"

"I think it was the puppy's angel," said Gary.

Whether it was his angel or the puppy's who orchestrated the rescue, it was a miracle.

When he brought the tiny canine home, Gary's wife, Lois, and daughter, sixteen-year-old Hannah, gushed over the fuzzy bundle, a teddy bear of a dog they could cradle in their arms like a baby. Hannah christened him Track and pleaded with her parents to keep him.

Lois shook her head and reminded her that they were already a three-dog family. Hannah, an animal lover and shelter volunteer, had recently become attached to one of the shelter's puppies. Scamps was a darling white lab, and she had convinced her parents to adopt him.

They would find Track a good home, Lois vowed. Meanwhile, Scamps and the thawed-out puppy became buddies, playing and sleeping together.

Lois contacted James Spann, an ABC weatherman for their local television affiliate, and asked if he could post a plea for homes on his

Gary McLean poses with Track, the puppy he rescued on an icy morning. (Photo by Lois McLean)

online blog. "He said it wasn't something he normally did but that he would make an exception since the story was weather related," Lois told me.

The blog posting soon attracted the attention of reporters, and Track's heartwarming tale was featured on local radio and TV.

"I ended up with about two hundred people who wanted to adopt him," said Lois. She carefully pored over the requests and finally settled on a woman who could give the puppy a "forever home."

People and pets take turns helping each other. When Diana Page Jordan, a Portland, Oregon, award-winning broadcast journalist, opened her home to a kitten in need, they ended up saving each other's lives.

I asked Diana to share the story of her miracle, and she provided the following.

Scamps greets his new friend. (Photo by Lois McLean)

Jet, My Lucky Black Cat
BY DIANA PAGE JORDAN

In the pitch black, I felt something soft on my right cheek. I brushed it away, smiling. I love the feel of fur against my bare skin. My cat Jet was lying next to me. Nine pounds, eleven ounces of big, black cat, he stretched long against me. He placed his paw gently on my cheek and stared into my eyes. His paw patted my cheek again.

The first time I saw him, he had no name. I was walking around the block when my neighbor flew out of her house toward me. "I have a kitten," she said. "I have to adopt it out or take him to the pound."

"Okay, I'll tell you what," I said. "If I can think of a name right away for the kitten, I'll take him."

"Wait right here." She dashed into the house.

A moment later she placed a tiny, black furball into the crook of my arm. I looked at him and said, "Jet."

My neighbor gasped.

"Oh no!" I said.

So now, here he was, petting my cheek, again and again.

"What, Jet, what?" I asked through a mask of sleep, as if he could answer. But he did.

He pushed his nose against mine. I tilted my head to look at the clock. "For gosh sakes, Jet, it's freaking 3:45!" My head dropped back onto the pillow.

I am petite and dance three hours every day and am one of the least likely people to have diabetes type II, but I got bad news a few summers back when I switched doctors.

The doctor got the reading instantly and put her head in her hands. "Why are you not in a coma?" she asked quietly. "Your blood sugar is 454, nearly five times what it should be."

She prescribed insulin, explaining that I could also fall into a coma if my blood sugar dropped below 50. I would have to monitor it carefully.

The bed shuddered. Jet stretched tall. He put his paw on my face. He petted me, mewed, then petted again.

"Fine. I'll get up." I sighed, sat up slowly, and touched my feet to the floor. At least they seemed like my feet. I felt giggles rise up inside of me. Legs wobbly, I walked toward the bathroom and, out of habit, scooped up my blood sugar monitor.

Jet strutted after me and sat, watching me like it mattered. I pulled back the plunger next to my right index finger and tested the bead of blood. "42. Uh oh, Jet, we're in trouble."

My thoughts slowed and I laughed. I was vaguely aware that my situation was not funny. Jet meowed.

"Orange juice," I said. When I got to the kitchen, there was Jet, sitting near the fridge. I plucked the bottle of juice from the top shelf, shook it and gulped down as much as I could. Finally, the natural sugar of the orange juice righted me.

I scooped up Jet. Nine pounds, eleven ounces, he likes to be held like a baby. I nuzzled my nose against him, and a grateful tear slipped onto his silky black belly.

Diana Page Jordan cuddles Jet as he demonstrates his life-saving technique.
(Leslie Rule)

Animal Miracles in the News

A FINE-FEATHERED FRIEND

WILLIE THE PARROT was credited with saving the life of toddler Hannah Kuusk in November 2008 in Denver, Colorado. The two-year-old was eating breakfast when she choked on a Pop Tart.

Babysitter Megan Howard had ducked into the bathroom and was unaware of the child's predicament until her exotic pet started screeching. The lime green Quaker parrot, whose normal vocabulary includes some rude words and the phrase, "I love you," shrieked, "Mama! Baby!" and wildly flapped his wings.

Megan Howard told a reporter, "Willie started screaming like I'd never heard him scream before." She rushed from the bathroom to find the little girl turning blue. Megan performed the Heimlich maneuver on Hannah, who soon began breathing again.

Willie was awarded a Red Cross "Animal Lifesaver Award" in the spring of 2009. (Sources include MSNBC.)

GOOD BOY!

A CALVERT, MARYLAND, woman owes her life to her dog, reported Elkton, Maryland's *Cecil Whig*. The two-year-old golden retriever named Toby performed the canine version of the Heimlich maneuver on Debbie Parkhurst, forty-five, when she choked on a bite of an apple on March 23, 2007.

She had tried unsuccessfully to perform the Heimlich on herself and then desperately beat on her own chest as she continued to choke. Toby got up on his hind legs, placed his paws on his mistress's shoulders, and knocked her to the floor. He jumped up and down on her chest until the apple dislodged from her throat.

The jewelry artist told reporters that the dog's lifesaving efforts left paw-shaped bruises on her chest.

GENTLE APE

ASTOUNDED ONLOOKERS at the Brookfield Zoo near Chicago, Illinois, watched as a three-year-old child fell into the ape enclosure on August 16, 1996, and was carried to safety by a nurturing female gorilla.

The little blond boy had climbed over a fence and fallen about twenty feet onto the concrete below and was knocked unconscious. Eight-year-old Binti Jua, with her own baby riding her back, scooped up the child and carried him away from the other apes, growling protectively as one approached. She placed him gently in the doorway, where zookeepers could reach him.

Binti Jua is the niece of Koko, the famous ape who gained worldwide media attention in the 1970s when she was taught to use the American Sign Language. (Koko was very gentle and had her own pet kitten.) Koko, living in the Gorilla Foundation in Woodside, California, was shown footage of her niece rescuing the little boy and was asked what she thought. In her own language, Koko replied "girl" and "good." (Sources include *The Chicago Tribune.*)

SMART DOG

MARY PHILLIPS, fifty-six, a nursing supervisor at Barnes–Jewish Hospice Care in St. Louis, Missouri, called pooch Jacque Pierre a "miracle" when he convinced her to seek medical attention after she ignored the advice of fellow nurses.

Mary was on the phone on October 27, 2008, when she was struck by a severe headache and decided to lie down on the floor. Alarmed employees urged her to go to he hospital, but she wouldn't listen until coworker Pat Harlan's poodle–Maltese mix began frantically licking her right temple.

A trip to the emergency room revealed an aneurysm the size of a walnut. Two months after surgery, she was back at work and grateful to the little white dog. Before her rescue, Mary was devoted to cats but had little patience for dogs and just "tolerated" her coworker's pet, who responded by ignoring her—until the day he zeroed in on her aneurysm. (Sources include *St. Louis Post–Dispatch*.)

(Leslie Rule)

HORSE HERALDED AS HERO

BBC News REPORTED that a Scottish woman, attacked by a cow, was rescued by her horse in August 2007. Fiona Boyd, forty, was attempting to reunite a lost calf with its mother on Chapmanton Farm in Castle Douglas, Scotland, when the mother cow became alarmed at the sound of her baby's frightened bellows and rammed the woman, knocking her down. "Every time I tried to crawl away, the cow just slammed into me again," Boyd told a reporter.

She was crumpled to the ground, certain her life was over, when her fifteen-year-old chestnut mare, Kerry, galloped to the rescue. Kerry had been grazing in a nearby field and rushed to defend her owner.

The cow retreated when the heroic horse charged her. Boyd suffered bad bruises and sore muscles but was otherwise fine.

HEAD OF THE CLASS

A TWO-YEAR-OLD HOUND named Hunter became a hero in December 2009 in Port St. Lucie, Florida, when he led his owner to a dying child.

When Reyna Zurita arrived home and opened the door, her recently adopted dog rushed out. She chased the dog for almost half a mile as he ignored her pleas for him to stop. Finally, he ran into a stranger's yard and stopped beside an unconscious infant.

Reyna leapt into action and performed CPR on the baby, whom she described as "purple, bleeding, and tight." The baby's caretaker said she had been bathing him when he slipped beneath the water and lost consciousness, so she had deposited him on the lawn and was off looking for help when Reyna and Hunter found him.

Paramedics soon took over Reyna's efforts, and officials said the baby was doing fine. Before Reyna adopted him, Hunter had been trained in a child rescue program but flunked because of poor performance. (Sources include *ABC News.*)

Author's note: The mysterious dog in the following case may have run away from his home because he was driven by the same psychic force that compelled Hunter to rescue the baby. It is possible he sensed the trouble hours before it occurred and traveled many miles to help.

A HERO APPEARED

A YOUNG FLORIDA MOTHER was threatened by a knife-wielding stranger in a park, only to be rescued by a stray dog who suddenly appeared on the scene. The mother and her two-year-old son were leaving the playground area in Higgs Park in Port Charlotte, Florida, in November 2008 when the culprit confronted them in the parking lot.

The thug turned on his heels when the sixty-five-pound bulldog–pit bull mix chased him, barking ferociously in an obvious show of defending the victims. The woman hurried to her car, but before she could drive away, the dog she called her "guardian angel" leapt into the backseat and sat down as if he belonged there.

Authorities believed that the well-fed dog, nicknamed "Angel" was probably recently lost, but when no one came forward to claim him, a Michigan pit bull rescue group took him in. (Sources include *NBC2 News.*)

DOG SAVES CAT

A PUG in West Billings, Montana, saved the life of her best friend, Willow the cat, on February 25, 2009. Chris Rubich, a writer for *The Billings Gazette,* reported that the one-year-old Siamese cat had fallen into a hole in the iced-over koi pond in her owner's backyard and had been paddling furiously for an estimated twenty minutes before she was found.

Seven-year-old Chloe was inside the home when Willow fell through the ice, but the pug seemed to sense that something was wrong. The little dog whimpered at the back door, and the unsuspecting owner, Amanda Bejelland, let her outside. The dog's incessant barking prompted her to let her back in, but she would not settle down.

Finally, Amanda realized that Chloe might be trying to tell her something and allowed her to lead her to the pond, where she found Willow, desperately paddling in the icy water. She immediately fished the cat out and took her indoors to warm up.

Chloe was rewarded with a bone.

DOG ON A MISSION

A YAMHILL, OREGON, dachshund named Missy who normally never left her yard ran a block for help after her owner, Charlie Burdon, collapsed inside his home while he was recovering from open heart surgery in August 2010.

The eleven-year-old wiener dog approached her owner's friend, Charles Mitchell, who was working in his yard. Missy refused to budge when Mitchell urged her to go home.

The behavior was so unusual that Mitchell followed Missy to the Burdons' home, where he found his friend and called paramedics. Charlie Burdon had suffered a dizzy spell but soon recovered. Both men agreed that Missy was a hero. (Sources include Portland, Oregon's *KATU TV News*.)

MIRACLE DOWN UNDER

A GENTLE DOG named Rex was out on a walk with his owner, Leonie Allan, in Torquay, Victoria, Australia, in the spring of 2008 when they passed a dead kangaroo on the side of the road. When they returned home, Rex, a cross between a German shorthaired and wire-haired pointer, began to point and then took off on his own.

He soon returned, tenderly carrying a four-month-old joey, who had survived when its mother was hit by a car. The ten-year-old dog had somehow sensed that life stirred within the mortally wounded kangaroo's pouch and managed to remove the baby kangaroo and bring him home.

The joey, soon christened Rex Jr. after his hero, formed a quick bond with the dog, hopping around him. Rex, in turn, licked his charge.

Authorities at Jirrahlinga Wildlife Sanctuary took the joey in with plans to release him back to the wild at the age of eighteen months. They expressed amazement at the cross-species friendship and at the success of the rescue, noting that many humans accidentally harm joeys when they drop the wriggling creatures. (Sources include Britain's *Daily Mail* and *The Telegraph*.)

A FISH OUT OF WATER

WHEN AN ENGLISH WOMAN found her pet goldfish floating on his side in his tank, she was certain he was dead. Carol Norris, Darren Bradnick, and their eighteen-year-old daughter, Ammba Bradnick, had welcomed Mr. Fish into their family thirteen years earlier when a then five-year-old Ammba won him at a fair.

In March 2010, Carol Norris, who lives in the Cambridge, England, area, plucked the floating fish from the water and gently wrapped him in tissue. She planned to have a proper burial for him later in the day and put him in the empty bathtub and then shut the bathroom door so the cats could not get to him.

Seven hours later she picked him up, and he flipped in her hand. She hurried to put him back in the water and was relieved to see that he was soon back to his old self. Experts suggested that the wet tissue may have provided enough oxygen to keep him alive, but the family called it a miracle. (Sources include Britain's *Daily Mail*.)

MR. HAMSTER'S WILD RIDE

IN JUNE 2006, *The BBC News* reported that workers at the Sandycroft, Wales, Recyclo recycling plant were stunned to find a live hamster on a conveyor belt, exiting machinery designed to rip refrigerators and other appliances to shreds. The fluffy, light brown hamster escaped unscathed with the exception of a sore foot and was soon adopted by ten-year-old Liam Bull, son of a Recyclo employee.

Mike the hamster apparently arrived in one of the many boats that deliver about 400 tons of dry waste daily to the Flintshire County plant.

A wild four-minute ride took the friendly rodent through the shredder and over a series of conveyor belts and vibrating grids and tumbled him in a huge rotating drum. Washing machines and other appliances emerge as metal ribbons, but the hamster miraculously survived.

ANGEL OF THE RIVER

AN EYEWITNESS to an extraordinary rescue of a drowning dog told reporters that help came in the form of a "guardian angel" who surfaced in time to save the canine's life. Chris Hinds, forty-three, and his teenage son, Raymond, were walking their dogs near the River Tees in northeast England's town of Middlesbrough in the spring of 2002 when they spotted an injured shepherd–lab mix.

When Chris approached to offer assistance, the dog panicked and jumped into the rushing water, which instantly carried him away. The would-be rescuer watched helplessly, certain the poor pooch was doomed. But the floundering dog's yelps alerted a seal, who emerged from the depths and then circled the struggling animal before nudging it to shore.

The dog was saved, Chris Hinds told a reporter, "in a matter of seconds."

Once the dog was safe on shore, three more seals surfaced and appeared to be "keeping an eye" on him.

Firefighters from the Stockton Fire Station captured the dog and found he had an injured leg and a gash on his head. (Sources include *BBC News* and *The Telegraph*.)

FIERCE PROTECTORS

A KIDNAPPED CHILD was rescued by three lions in the spring of 2005. The twelve-year-old Ethiopian girl had been abducted by a group of men who planned to force her into marriage. The terrified girl was held captive in a remote corner of Ethiopia for seven days, until the lions appeared and chased away her startled kidnappers.

Meanwhile, the girl's family and police were in pursuit and eventually discovered the weeping victim. Sgt. Wondimu Wedajo told a reporter that the magnificent felines had stood guard over the girl for half a day and trotted off once help arrived. He added that "they left her like a gift" before they disappeared into the jungle.

Wildlife expert Stuart Williams suggested that the girl's whimpers may have sounded like a mewing cub to the lions and inspired a protective instinct. (Sources include *BBC News*.)

A lion with angel wings guards the entryway of a 1924 building at 215 Columbia Street in downtown Seattle, Washington. (Leslie Rule)

Chapter Twelve
CHRISTMAS MIRACLES

LOVE CAME DOWN AT CHRISTMAS;
LOVE ALL LOVELY, LOVE DIVINE;
LOVE WAS BORN AT CHRISTMAS,
STARS AND ANGELS GAVE THE SIGN.

—*Christina G. Rossetti,* ENGLISH POET (1830–1894)

Four days before Christmas, a few years back when I was living
in Puyallup, Washington, my telephone rang and I answered to hear
an operator ask if I would accept a collect call from Pierce County
jail inmate Amy Olson.★

I didn't know her, but I did not hesitate. I accepted the call.

★Name changed to protect her privacy.

I was soon talking to a young woman who had dialed my number by mistake. She had been arrested and was hoping that a friend would bail her out of jail, and she had been trying to phone him when she misdialed.

She explained that her parents always let their answering machine pick up their calls. She had no way to contact them because inmates must call collect, and her parents' answering machine could not accept the charges.

She tearfully told me her story. She was twenty and had been staying with friends who had left their drugs and drug paraphernalia in the window of their house, in clear view of a police officer who happened by. She had been in trouble in the past, she told me, emphasizing that this time the drugs were not hers.

I believed her. But it would not have mattered to me if the drugs *were* hers. She was frightened and she was alone. My heart went out to her as she sobbed, "I don't want to spend Christmas in jail!"

I offered to call the friend that she'd been trying to reach and to phone her parents and leave a message on their machine. "Please call me and let me know what happens," I said. "And you can call me collect if you want to talk again."

She thanked me and gave me the phone numbers. I called the friend first, noting that his number was very close to mine. Amy had transposed two of the digits and reached me instead. He was more of an acquaintance than a friend, she had said, but she thought he could afford to bail her out. I was not surprised when he ignored the message I left on his answering machine.

Her parents lived in Eatonville, Washington, a city in the foothills of Mount Rainier, about thirty miles from my home. I knew the area. In fact, my then husband and I owned a cabin on wooded acreage in Eatonville. I spent little time there, but my ex stayed there often.

I called Amy's parents and left a detailed message on their machine. Amy called me several times over the next couple of days. She was still in jail, still scared and very depressed about being in a cold, gray cell during the holidays. I don't remember exactly what we talked about. But I do remember her small voice, always relieved when I accepted her calls.

My then husband had been staying at our cabin for the past few days, and when he returned, I told him the story of Amy. His jaw dropped. Amy and her family lived next door to our property, he told me. Though I had never met them, he knew them well. He was astounded by the coincidence.

What were the odds that Amy would reach me by accident?

I'm not sure how many people would accept a collect call from a stranger in prison. When I accepted the call, I knew the caller had misdialed. I was compelled by curiosity, by compassion, and by the fact that I believe that just as there are no coincidences, there are no wrong numbers!

On Christmas Eve, Amy called again. This time it was *not* a collect call. She wanted to thank me and to let me know that she was home with her parents for Christmas. She, too, was surprised to learn of the "coincidence" in our odd connection.

I never spoke with Amy again, but I heard that she straightened out her life and that she is a mother now. I also heard that her family refers to me as "Amy's Angel."

I'm no angel, but I wonder if a *real* angel orchestrated the telephone encounter that resulted in Amy going home for Christmas.

While a "wrong number" defied the odds when it connected Amy and me, another case defied physics. Ted Whitford of Vancouver, Washington, sent me the following letter about his Christmas miracle.

I was a sophomore in college in Washington, D.C. My buddy, Eric Stuyck, invited me to spend Christmas vacation with his family in Vermont. During that vacation, Eric's car left the roadway, and we slid through a farmer's field of snow and ice. During the slide, the gigantic tree looming in front of us was at times head on, and at times it was on the left and then on the right.

The car slammed against the tree, and the farmer came out of his house. After the impact, I asked Eric if he was okay, and he asked me the same. I remember the farmer assessing the situation and scratching his head.

You see, the tire tracks led directly to the tree. The car, however, was on the opposite side of the tree. The farmer was confused because the tire tracks went right to the tree, with the car on the other side. It appeared that we had traveled through the tree.

During Christmas break last year, while I was taking my sophomore son to Washington State University in Pullman, Washington, he asked about God's purpose for our lives. I recounted the story about the tree and said, "If my life purpose was to live to the point where I was able to have created you, I will be proud to say that I have fulfilled my life's purpose."

We were both choked up for a moment. I truly believe that the accident in 1981 was a miracle.

A wrong number gone right. A car traveling *through* a tree as if it were made of mist. Both are Christmas miracles. In the first instance a distraught young woman found her way home, and in the second, lives were spared.

Divine intervention is especially sweet at Christmas time. Grief, too, can be more profound during the sentimental season. The women in the following story thought nothing could ease the pain in their hearts—until they met a band of angels.

Mystery Shoppers

Jonathan was a joyful child who loved to laugh. He looked a little like an angel, with his head of golden curls and wide, innocent eyes. The toddler was blissfully unaware of his serious health problems.

"He was born with Goldenhar syndrome," confided his grandmother, Nancy Fischer, of Lake Canandaigua, New York. She explained that the syndrome divided his body down the middle from his head to his waist, with one half functioning normally and the opposite side plagued with cranial and vertebral deformities. The features on half of his face were malformed, but those who loved him saw only his beautiful spirit.

Jonathan's mother, Cheri Smith, worried about his future. Doctors had told her that the little boy would have to endure many surgeries in the years to come. Both she and her mother, Nancy, prayed he would not suffer.

In June 1998 Jonathan was just eighteen months old when a complication related to his condition suddenly and unexpectedly took his life. Mother and daughter fell into each other's arms. They grieved for the little boy but vowed to accept his death as a blessing. They knew his spirit was intact and that they would one day see him again. They took comfort in the fact that Jonathan would never have to face another painful procedure.

Cheri knew she had to go on for Jonathan's baby brother, four-month old Andrew, and she tried to be strong, but the next months were tough. As Christmas approached, the sadness deepened.

"We couldn't help thinking of the year before, when Jonathan was with us," Cheri told me. "Mom was trying to cheer me up and suggested that we go Christmas shopping." Though her heart wasn't in it, Cheri went along.

Christmas music wafted through the large discount store as Cheri strapped Andrew into a cart. The women meandered down an aisle, trying to get enthused about the merchandise.

"We noticed two people walking toward us," said Nancy. "They were pushing carts and smiling at us and looking at us with such loving eyes."

Nancy and Cheri returned the smiles, thinking of little Jonathan as they noticed that the shoppers had facial birth defects. "We had such a tenderness for that," said Nancy. "We turned a corner and saw another person with a birth defect. And then we saw *another!*"

Cheri and Nancy glanced at each other. "It was very strange," said Nancy. "Everywhere we looked we saw someone with a disability. They were all smiling at us."

With each corner they turned, they encountered another shopper with a facial distortion who gazed at them with an innocent joy.

"I wondered if they were with a group," Nancy remembered. "I thought they might be on an outing. I looked around but didn't see a nurse or an assistant."

"We saw at least fifteen people over the next fifteen minutes," said Cheri, explaining that each one had the same special quality. And each one met their eyes and smiled warmly.

The women were perplexed by the unusual situation, but they continued to shop. As they went down the toy aisle, Cheri spotted something that Jonathan would have enjoyed.

With a lump in her throat, she walked on by and was just about to exit the aisle when a man pushed his shopping cart in her path.

"He *blocked* our way!" Cheri told me. Nancy and Cheri watched the man, wondering what he was up to. "He was short and bald and looked to be about sixty," said Cheri. "He had the most beautiful eyes I've ever seen. He stood there for the longest time."

Cheri stared back at him, mesmerized by the deep blue eyes that seemed to see right into her soul. Finally he spoke, his words carefully measured. "I just wanted to wish you a merry Christmas," he said.

Cheri and Nancy were instantly struck by the same realization: *He is an angel!*

Neither spoke the words out loud, but each knew the man was not of this earth. "I was afraid to look at Mom because I knew I'd start crying," said Cheri.

The women were too dumbstruck to speak as they watched the fellow turn away. "I took my eyes off him for just a second, and when I looked back he was gone," said Cheri. "We looked for him. I was actually running through the store, trying to find him." But the "man" had vanished.

No human being could have disappeared in the brief moment the women had looked away. Still, they searched. "We even went outside and looked in the parking lot," said Cheri.

"All the others were gone too," said Nancy, adding that the store was once again filled with regular folks. Though the special people had been pushing shopping carts of merchandise, not a single one was in line at the checkout counter. Each one had vanished as mysteriously as the man who had blocked their path.

"We left our carts and went out to the car," said Nancy. "There was no way we could shop after that. We had realized we'd met an angel at the same moment," she added, describing the calm certainty that had washed over them. And they did not doubt that the others were angels, sent to them with a message. And that message was clear.

Jonathan was okay.

He was in a better place. Though they had believed it before, now their faith was renewed. Angels had appeared on his behalf.

Just as they had instinctively known that the mystery shoppers were angels, the women were certain of their message. "That is when the healing began," said Cheri.

Today Cheri is the mother of four healthy children. She has shown Jonathan's siblings the photo albums filled with pictures of the joyful brother they will never know. And when Cheri and Nancy look at the photographs of the laughing child, they smile. They still miss him but know that they will see him again.

Angels bring gifts of all kinds. When they appeared in the store, they delivered a gift of joy, replacing the grief that ravaged the hearts of the two women who so loved the little boy with the short and difficult life. Sent by God and hand delivered by angels who knew just how to appear to reach the women weighted down by sadness, the message was salve on their wounds.

A Nova Scotia couple thought they had all the gifts they needed, wrapped and layered beneath their tree. There was, however, one gift not on their list. It did not even occur to them to ask for it, but when they received it, they knew it was the best gift ever.

The Christmas Gift

The MacDonalds were ready for Christmas. It was December 24, 2010, and Margaret and her husband, Andrew, were enjoying a quiet evening in their Glace Bay, Nova Scotia, home. Andrew sat at the computer in the kitchen while Margaret was down the hall, relaxing in her office as she read a book.

They looked forward to Christmas morning, when their grown daughter and other relatives would gather at their home to exchange gifts. Presents were piled beneath the tree that Margaret had purchased a month earlier and decorated with a string of bright little lights and dozens of ornaments.

Margaret's two favorite ornaments sat atop a little table in the hallway. Both were angels, about six inches tall. She loved angels, and the pair were her prized possessions. She sometimes joked with Andrew that the figurines were their guardian angels, looking over them.

As Margaret and Andrew were winding down that Christmas Eve, their lapdogs, Daisy the Chihuahua, Tiana the shih tzu, and Pookie the Pomeranian, were resting, but their boxer, Roxy, was acting strangely.

The couple had adopted Roxy nearly fifteen years earlier, when she was a pudgy puppy. "I've always had a special connection with her," Margaret confided. "I've been closer to her than to any other pet."

The brown and white dog with the friendly and relaxed demeanor was eerily in tune with Margaret. "I suffered from vertigo a while back," she said, describing how the inner ear disorder made her so dizzy it was difficult to walk.

Roxy seemed to sense something was wrong the morning the episodes began. Margaret was still in bed when Roxy walked up and slipped her head beneath her mistress's hand. "My hand touched her collar," said Margaret. "She was letting me know that I could hold onto her so she could guide me."

The MacDonalds worried about the elderly dog, who had developed arthritis and seemed to be in pain. A few months earlier, they had brought Roxy to the vet, and Margaret braced herself for the doctor's verdict. "I was afraid he was going to tell me that it was time to put her down. But instead he put her on medicine and told us she had more time with us."

She was grateful that Roxy was still with them that Christmas Eve but was admittedly a little annoyed as the old dog paced restlessly. Margaret was trying to read, but Roxy was ambling back and forth between her office and the living room and making odd grunting noises.

"Roxy, what do you want?" asked Margaret.

The behavior was so unusual that she finally put down her book and followed the dog down the hall to the living room. "Roxy wouldn't let me go into the room," she said. The boxer blocked the doorway, her brown eyes fixed upon the Christmas tree.

Margaret MacDonald hugs Roxy, her best friend and savior, as Daisy looks on. (Photo by Andrew MacDonald)

Margaret followed her gaze. "The tree was lit up and looked pretty," she said. "I was staring at it when I saw a little flash of light, like lightning."

She wondered for a moment if she had imagined it, but then she saw it *again*. But before she could make sense of what she was seeing, the tree went up in flames.

"It went 'poof,'" she said. Flames shot across the ceiling as Margaret screamed, "Run!"

The command both startled and confused Andrew, who was still sitting at the computer, but when he heard his wife shout, "The house is on fire!" he leapt from his chair and joined her as she raced toward the back door with all four dogs at her heels.

"We couldn't get out the door!" said Margaret. "It was just a metal screen door and usually opens easily, but it wouldn't open even though Andrew was pounding on it."

Thick, acrid smoke enveloped them, and Margaret cried, "God, please don't let us die!"

At that instant, the door popped open. Andrew pushed his wife outside, and the dogs tumbled after her. He glanced back to see a ball of fire roaring down the hall toward them.

The couple and their animals made it to safety. They watched from the sidewalk, in shock. Their picture window glowed with orange light, and they heard the disconcerting noise of crackles and pops as the flames devoured their home.

They had thought that they were prepared for the possibility of a fire. Smoke detectors were installed throughout the house, and they routinely checked the batteries. They had even purchased an escape ladder for the upstairs bedroom.

The tree lights were several years old, but Margaret had carefully examined them for wear and tear before stringing them on the tree. The defect, she learned later, was hidden within the casing.

"The smoke detectors didn't have time to go off," said Margaret. "They instantly melted into balls of plastic and fell to the floor."

The firefighters explained to the MacDonalds that the fire had sucked up the oxygen, creating a vacuum effect. "That's why we couldn't get the door open," Margaret said. The suction was so powerful, it not only held the door shut, it pulled the screws from the grip rock walls.

The flash fire had shot through the MacDonalds' home, incinerating its contents. Margaret and Andrew boarded the three small dogs at a kennel and found a hotel that would accept Roxy.

Though blackened by the fire, Margaret's prized angel figurines inexplicably survived intact. (Photo by Margaret MacDonald)

They did not want to be separated from the dog who had saved their lives.

They checked into the hotel wearing their smoke-damaged clothing. They knew they had much to be thankful for. They had survived. Miraculously their pets, too, had escaped.

The little dogs often reacted nervously to stressful situations. Margaret thanked God that they hadn't cowered beneath a couch instead of chasing her out the door.

The MacDonalds counted their blessings. Yet it was a shock to realize their worldly possessions were gone. Two days later, they visited the site of the destruction. The walls were black and charred, their furniture was ashes. Margaret was nauseous as she looked around at what had once been her lovely home.

It seemed that all their worldly goods were gone. But then she discovered that two objects had survived the fire. Margaret's prized angel figurines were intact. Though stained with smoke, they were whole.

"Everything else was destroyed," said Margaret. The figurines can be cleaned, she told me, but they will always smell of smoke. She plans to have them encased in glass and forever keep them near. For they are a reminder of the Christmas miracle that delivered the best gift ever: their lives.

Christmas Miracles in the News

ANGEL COME HOME

A CAT NAMED ANGEL was the star of a Colorado family's very own Christmas miracle according to a December 24, 2004, issue of the *Aspen Times*. Journalist Janet Urquhart reported on the heartwarming case of a pretty white cat who vanished from his home at Christmastime five years earlier and was believed to be lost forever.

Sam Mosher told the reporter how she and her children, Lindsey and Parker, had adopted two cats, Fly and Angel, from an area shelter a decade before and were brokenhearted when Angel disappeared, apparently taken by a predator.

Five years passed, and it was one week before Christmas when twenty-two-year-old Lindsey dreamed of the long-lost Angel.

The next morning she picked up the latest edition of the *Aspen Times Weekly* and found herself staring at an image of a cat who looked just like their missing Angel. The photograph of the white cat with one blue and one green eye accompanied an article featuring adoptable shelter pets.

"By coincidence or miracle," wrote Janet Urquhart, "the cat was selected over other pets in the shelter's care for the photograph."

Lindsey sprang into action and soon learned that the cat had been found in the area at the same time Angel went missing and was taken in by a married couple. After the wife died, the husband took the cat to the shelter.

Shelter workers noted that the underfed feline was very shy, but he perked up as Lindsey called, "Angel!" Angel dashed over to her and began purring.

Angel not only remembered her humans, she was also happy to see Fly. The reporter quoted Lindsey: "Once they got together, they were making little cat-chat sounds at each other."

JOSEPH AND MARY

A VERNON, FLORIDA, woman was taking a drive with her boyfriend in mid-December 1995 when a chance stop at a park turned into a Christmas miracle. Debby Brewer went into the boat ramp restroom at the Lake Powell Recreation Area, about twenty miles west of Panama City, and heard soft crying. When she investigated, she discovered twin babies inside a duffel bag.

Panama City Police Lieutenant Jerry Girvin told reporters that it was a miracle the infants were found alive. Though the isolated park was used by fishermen in the summer, it was mostly deserted in the winter. The babies, just thirty-six hours old, would not have survived long in the cold restroom.

When the story made headlines, 650 people offered to adopt the babies, who were nicknamed Mary and Joseph because they were found so close to Christmas. (Sources include *The Sitka Sentinel*.)

HAND OF GOD

A SECURITY, COLORADO, woman died during labor, and her baby appeared to be stillborn on Christmas Eve in 2009, but their story took a miraculous turn.

Thirty-five-year-old Tracy Hermanstorfer was holding hands with her husband, Mike, thirty-seven, and discussing baby names when her heart stopped. Doctors and nurses at Memorial Hospital in Colorado Springs, Colorado, tried to revive her as her shocked husband watched.

Dr. Stephanie Martin said, "She was dead. She had no heartbeat. No breathing. She was as gray as her sweat suit."

Concerned for the unborn baby's safety, doctors rushed Tracy into surgery. They performed a cesarean section and delivered a limp baby boy. Mike Hermanstorfer held his tiny son as doctors worked on him, trying to get him to breathe.

The young father thought he had lost everything when an astounding thing occurred. His wife's heart started beating *and* the infant stirred to life.

Doctors were baffled by the entire incident and could not say why she died or why she came back to life, but Mike Hermanstorfer called his family's revival "an absolute miracle." (Sources include *The Denver Post* and *The New York Daily News*.)

WATCHERS IN THE NIGHT

ANGELS HELPED A THREE-YEAR-OLD survive an accident that took his mother's life on Christmas Eve in 2001, near Joggins, Cumberland County, Nova Scotia. The Halifax *Daily News* reported that Gage Gabriel was discovered shivering and wet on the rocky beach beside the Bay of Fundy.

Tobi Gabriel lost her life when the car sailed off a cliff and landed upside down. Young Gage Gabriel survived with frostbitten toes and a lump on the head.

The child told an officer that he saw two women in white with wings who stood in the water and smiled at him all night long.

Roy Gabriel, the child's great-grandfather, said, "That's what kept him alive. If it wasn't for that, the boy would have died there in the rain."

SLEEPING BEAUTY

WHEN PATRICIA WHITE BULL woke up on Christmas Eve in 1999, her mother called it a "miracle from God." Sixteen years earlier, the Edgewood, New Mexico, woman was giving birth to her fourth child via a cesarean section when a blot clot in her lung cut off her oxygen. Patricia went into a catatonic state, and her family was told her condition was permanent.

The miracle occurred at Las Palomas Nursing and Rehabilitation Center in Albuquerque, where the patient was confined to a bed and fed through a tube. Though her eyes were open and she sometimes seemed to track people as they walked across the room, she did not respond to pain or appear to communicate.

Nurses were adjusting her sheets on Christmas Eve when Patricia suddenly said, "Don't do that." She was soon reunited with her family, eating pizza and walking. (Sources include the *Albuquerque Journal*.)

(Leslie Rule)

Author Leslie Rule would love to hear from readers
about the miracles in their lives. Please e-mail her at
Angels4Leslie@yahoo.com, or write her at:
Leslie Rule, 1916 Pike Place, Suite 12 #444, Seattle, WA 98101.

Leslie Rule is a professional photographer and the author of seven books
with paranormal themes. She also has written dozens of articles for national magazines, including *Reader's Digest*. The daughter of best-selling
true-crime author Ann Rule, Leslie grew up in a haunted house, where
her lifelong fascination with the paranormal began. She lives in the Seattle,
Washington, area.